Crazy Shortcut Quilts

Quilt as You Go and Finish in Half the Time!

Marguerita McManus & Sarah Raffuse

©2007 Marguerita McManus and Sarah Raffuse

Published by

krause publications

An Imprint of F+W Publications

700 East State Street • Iola, WI 54990-0001
715-445-2214 • 888-457-2873
www.krausebooks.com

Our toll-free number to place an order or obtain
a free catalog is (800) 258-0929.

All rights reserved. No portion of this publication may be
reproduced or transmitted in any form or by any means,
electronic or mechanical, including photocopy, recording,
or any information storage and retrieval system, without
permission in writing from the publisher, except by a
reviewer who may quote brief passages in a critical article
or review to be printed in a magazine or newspaper,
or electronically transmitted on radio, television, or the
Internet.

The following registered trademark terms and companies
appear in this publication: Insul-Bright®, Retayne™, Steam-
A-Seam 2®, Timtex™, Warm & Natural®, Warm & White®,
Sulky®, Goo Gone®, Sulky® of America, Coats and Clark Star®,
Synthrapol®.

Library of Congress Control Number: 2007923003

ISBN 13: 978-089689-547-8
ISBN 10: 0-89689-547-5

Designed by Katrina Newby
Edited by Tracy L. Conradt

Printed in China

Dedication

Without the loving fan club that we had in "the boys" we wouldn't even have tried half of the things we've done. Nothing could motivate us like the desire to hear their reactions to our endless new projects, and their unwavering support and enjoyment of life, which they are and were so much a part of.

Our dedication is to all people who have loved and lost a child to an untimely death. The loss we suffer, no one knows. The memories we cherish, worth more than anything. In loving memory of Mickey, Joey and Christopher Woods, our nephews and cousins - the lights of our lives.

Contents

Contents

Special Thanks

Some people are such an inspiration that their faces and voices are a part of our lives and memories forever. Their laughs, their smiles, their encouraging words, the warmth of presence of their hands on our shoulders keep us moving forward.

The encouragement of Karen Tomzcak, whose incredible drive and savvy has motivated many Alaskan quilters, and the example and inspiration of Dina Pappas and Trish Stewart have kept us trying new things and loving every minute of it. We are grateful to you all. Marguerita especially thanks Tom Buchanan for his help creating the quilts and aunts Doris, Carol and Marie, who "showed me the world and I am grateful every day. It's funny how people who expect the most of me, inspire me to search out and give the best that I have to offer."

Sarah would like to give special thanks to her husband Ryan, and to Beth Gold, Laura McDonell and Jeanne South – you guys are my quilting inspiration.

We both thank RJR Fabrics and Robert Kaufman Fabrics for their gorgeous contributions of fabrics for the quilts; Sulky of America for their threads and Maret Anderson and her staff at Seams Like Home Quilt Shoppe in Anchorage. We are grateful to Katie Newby for her wonderful design work; Kris Kandler for her patience and outstanding photography and especially to Candy Wiza and our editor, Tracy Conradt, at Krause Publications who have given us this wonderful opportunity to write this book.

Introduction

We love a great shortcut when traveling, cooking and quilting, since it usually takes us on a path less traveled and often saves us time. Crazy Shortcut Quilts has an amazing combination of short steps and has eliminated tasks in quilt making, allowing you to finish your quilt in record time, even if you've never quilted before!

Old fashioned quilters used small scraps of leftover or recycled fabrics, then hand or machine sewed the pieces together, using old blankets as filling, hand quilting needlework or yarn ties to secure the layers. Today's quilters have available fabrics of the finest quality, specialized battings and computerized sewing machines to make their quilts. Still it's a struggle to complete a quilt because of the traditional process of piecing the whole top and layering it with bed-sized batting and an oversized backing before beginning the quilting – the process of joining the three layers.

Traditional crazy quilts involve an additional step because once the pieces of fabrics are joined, decorative stitching is added. It makes an elegant and always unique quilt, but often takes months if not years to make.

We have a new way of making these lovely, unique and sophisticated quilts, in much less time than the traditional method! Making a Crazy Shortcut Quilt is exciting for experienced quilters, non-quilters and new quilters because there is virtually no precise measuring or cutting!

Your sewing machine and it's decorative stitches do all of the quilting in small, manageable sections – no quilting skills needed, no struggling to quilt a huge quilt in a sewing machine, no need to hire a professional quilter!

We help you choose fabrics that coordinate with your home décor or add a decorative spice to existing room décor, making every project truly a designer crazy quilt.

If you know nothing at all about quilt making – relax! Sarah's been teaching the technique for years to absolute beginners, who often finish their projects in a single weekend! Now that's really taking a shortcut to a crazy quilt!

Our book assumes that you have never made a quilt before, and therefore we begin with basic how-to chapters that fully explain each part of the process. While we encourage everyone to read through all of the chapters, an experienced quilt maker who already has a color scheme in mind for her fabrics may choose to skip the beginning chapters and go right to The Shortcuts.

With each design we have given detailed information for fabric requirements and cutting, however, the designs are interchangeable! If you see a design you like but want to make a different size quilt than the size offered for that design, review all the chapters for the size quilt you want and purchase the fabrics as stated for that size quilt – but make the cuts according to the plan we give you for your chosen design.

We've divided the projects into sections based on some of our favorite cuts, and added a little lagniappe with accessorizing home décor projects that coordinate with your quilts.

We believe in the "keep it sweet and simple" philosophy so we'll give you the short version here:

✂ Starting with squares (sometimes rectangles) of fabrics, make straight cuts, re-sew the pieces without matching fabrics and repeat as necessary for your project

✂ Layer each square (or rectangle) for quilting and decoratively stitch along the seam lines, changing threads and/or stitching designs as desired

✂ Trim, sash together and bind your crazy quilted squares

The projects are so easy and quick that we describe them like this:

Crazy quilts that you can make in a very

Short time using a few straight

Cuts and decoratively stitched into gorgeous décor

Quilts! Let's get started!

CHAPTER [1]   Getting Started

There are just a few things that you'll need to make your quilt, and a few things you won't need! You don't need any quilt-making experience at all. In fact, we don't follow some of the rules of traditional quilt making and that's one of our first shortcuts!

You'll need a sewing machine with at least one decorative stitch, even if it is just a simple zigzag zag stitch. Don't worry if you don't have a machine with 1,000 stitches. We can show you how to get about 30 different looks from 13 simple decorative stitches. We also show you a quilt that uses lots of threads and only one decorative stitch – and it is quite elegant!

You'll need fabric, batting and threads. We're going to give you every tip we know of to help you select materials you will be happy with and that have worked well for us for years. We've had a lot of experience here and we've got some really unique methods. Trust us, they will work for you.

Other necessities are straight pins, safety pins, iron and pad or ironing board, rotary cutter and mat, and acrylic ruler – either two rulers which combined can measure 18" or the large 20½" square acrylic ruler. If you want to make the window valances you'll need a sew-through fabric stiffener, and a fusible web. If you choose to make the décor accent pillows, you'll need pillow forms for those projects.

The techniques we are going to teach you are ones that we've used for years. We'll tell you how to budget your time for your project and complete it in quick, easy sections.

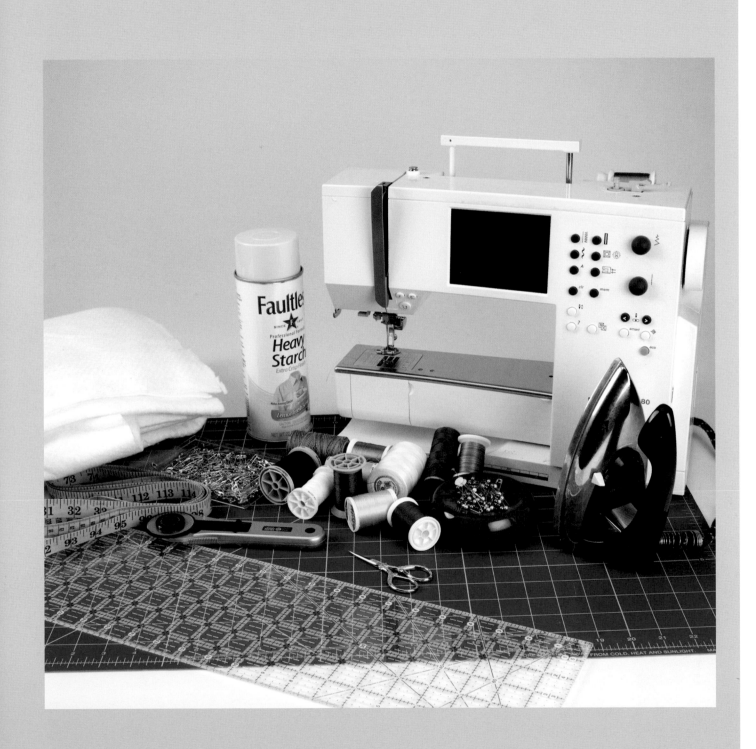

CHAPTER [2]
Crazy Ideas for Selecting Fabrics, Threads & More

Fabrics

Fabric selection can be very overwhelming, and like paint chips in a hardware store, hundreds of bolts of fabric can leave you frozen, staring and afraid to make the wrong choice. It can be difficult to get started with a single fabric selection and intimidating to add complementary fabrics to an initial fabric selection.

Some sewers find the fabric selection process so difficult, in fact, that they never get started with the project that they want to do! We have a few steps for you to take if you face any of these issues, and even if you select fabrics with ease, you might find an idea or two here that may inspire you to tweak your style just a little!

Don't let the vast selection intimidate you. We have advice to help you select fabrics that you'll love and work well together.

First, a little information about fabrics. Generally, fabrics are sold on the bolt (a cardboard insert used to wrap the fabric around it so that it stands nicely on a shelf) and in widths of 44" or so, folded in half to be 22" high. This is generally called yardage, and fabric is cut by measuring off as many yards of the 44" wide fabric as the shopper wants. If you ask for 1 yard, you will usually get a piece of fabric that is 44" wide and 36" long. So, a ½ yard would be 44" wide by 18" long, and ¼ yard would be 44" wide by 9" long.

Someone came up with a brilliant plan to just use half of the width of a ½-yard cut (making it 22" instead of 44") and called it a fat quarter. This is one of the most useful innovations in fabric cutting. It's a lot easier to use a piece of fabric that measures 22" x 18" than a strip that is 44" x 9", and they have the exact same amount of fabric.

Many fabric retailers make it easy to take advantage of this innovation by folding and matching coordinating fabrics into bundles, called fat quarter bundles. We love to buy fat quarter bundles for our projects and we encourage you to explore this option in your fabric shopping. Some retailers have even taken this one step further and have folded fabrics in fat eighths – a strip of fabric 9" x 22". We took advantage of this with the Fossil Fern Flannel Quilt and the Fast Friends Quilt. It saved one whole step in each project!

Selecting fabrics can be as easy as matching your focus fabric color to those of a fat quarter bundle!

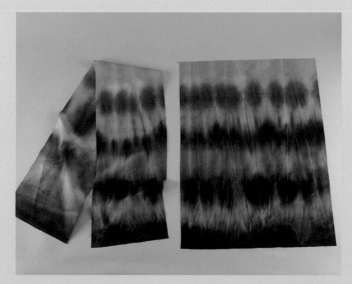

A fat quarter has the same amount of fabric as a standard ¼-yd. cut but in a much more usable size!

In the sashing chapter we make reference to the grain of the fabric. It is important to understand grain, so that you understand how fabric stretches. For example, with a one-yard cut which measures 44" x 36" you will have a selvage edge – a tightly woven edge with markings about the dyes used, color codes, designer and fabric manufacturer. When you pull gently on the fabric, with one hand on each selvage, you get some stretch. This direction, from selvage edge to selvage edge, is called the cross-wise grain. The length of the fabric, as it travels along the selvage edge, is called the lengthwise grain and it has very little stretch. These two facts can be very useful in planning your cutting and sewing pieces, especially in cutting the sashing.

If you angle from corner to corner of a square cut of fabric, you have what is called the "bias" or bias grain. This stretches more than any other direction – so when you cut and re-sew along that angle you need to be careful not to pull the fabrics as you sew.

The bias grain is the "stretchiest" of all.

Different fiber fabrics have different properties, and some stretch much more than others – making any project challenging. We have stayed with 100% cotton in all of our quilts. Wherever possible throughout the book we have given information about the manufacturer, line and name of the fabrics we used for each quilt project shown, as well as our thread selections.

Each project gives generous fabric requirements. Consider combining several projects to create a special and unique fabric décor for your home.

You will also see references to terms like

Top – the traditional single layer of fabric on the top of a quilt

Back or Backing – the fabric used for the bottom or back side of the quilt

Batting – the fill layer of insulation between the top and back of the quilt

Sashing – the strips used to connect blocks or squares of fabric on the top or back

Binding – the strips of fabric used to finish off the edges of the quilt

Quilting – the process of joining with thread the three layers of the quilt

Square - for our purposes we use the term square even if your project is made with rectangles. Traditional quilt making calls the small project a block and it is sewn very precisely and in a very different manner than we use for our quilts. For that reason, we prefer to call our cutting projects squares instead of blocks.

Selecting Fabrics that will work for you

Crazy Idea #1 – Pick a room in your home that you will make this quilt for, then select an item from the room that has a color that you particularly like. Look at wall color, window treatment fabrics, sofa coverings or bedding. Perhaps choose a vase, lamp base, book cover or some artwork that has a particular color that you love.

If possible, take the item (photo frame, pillowcase, swatch of drapery fabric, swatch of carpet) with you to your fabric shop and use it to select your focus fabric. Sarah used the protective cover from the arm of her sofa for color inspiration for one quilt – she just slid it off the sofa and went shopping! If it's not possible to bring your inspiration item (like your whole sofa!) with you, look for a paint chip that matches the color. Many paint stores have cards with several shades of paint on one card and can be very handy to bring with you in helping you match fabric colors.

Bring something from home to help you select your fabrics.

Crazy Idea #2 – Select a theme, print, or element that can be carried through several fabrics – for instance, an outdoor theme. A green fabric printed with leaves combined with a reddish orange fabric or stone color fabric with brick, rocks or stones printed on it and matched with a sky blue fabric with a cloud theme and topped off with a brown or tan with wood grain makes for a super outdoor lover's quilt.

Follow the same theory with all types of fabric. Look for a print with a theme that you can repeat in other colors. Some fabric manufacturers will have a consistent print theme in many color ways – like decorative swirls in every color imaginable. A repeated theme might be bugs for a kids quilt. There are bug prints in every color and scale imaginable.

Another element might be a metallic imprint or shine to the fabric, and you can use gold, copper, silver and then match fabrics that complement that element to your quilt. Any of these ideas can make a good start for someone who's never picked out a fabric palette before.

Bug fabrics are always popular for a kid's quilt..

Holiday fabrics are great for Crazy Shortcut Quilts.

Crazy Idea #3 – Make a holiday quilt and use the fabric colors associated with that holiday, perhaps even a fabric printed with the holiday design. Christmas, Easter, Thanksgiving, and Halloween are holidays strongly associated with colors and can be a inspiration for you when selecting your fabrics.

Crazy Idea #4 – Start with just one color in mind, and then select one or more fabrics in the store that totally embrace that color. From here it's easy to add fabrics. Jump ahead to the section titled Adding to your Focus Fabric.

Crazy Idea #5 – Go into your fabric shop with a totally open mind and select a fabric that you fall in love with! Any fabric at all! Take a look at Sarah's Beautiful Batiks quilt and her notes on selecting the fabrics for her quilt. Notice how well the threadwork really stands out against the batik fabrics. This is one of the most fun ways to make your first Crazy Shortcut Quilt, especially if you intend to have the quilt be tossed into a mismatched décor or be given as a gift. This can be really fun to do with a baby quilt or a quilt meant for the back seat of a car or van. Really, you can't go wrong!

Crazy Idea #6 – Start with thread. Take a look at the gorgeous threads available today, especially the variegated threads, and select one that you really love. Select threads, darker and lighter that complement your selection. Now go through the fabric shop looking for fabrics that match the threads that you have selected! Remember that more complicated decorative stitching uses thread a lot faster than simple stitches.

Adding to your Focus Fabric

Building upon your focus fabric selection is the next step and it can be just as easy. Marguerita says, "One of my favorite things to do is to ask a friend whose eye for color I admire or ask for help from a fabric shop employee whose projects I admire. I love to look at quilts hanging in a quilt shop and ask which employee made them. From here, I just ask for help from that employee. The employee is happy to be flattered and usually loves fabric so much that she can show me several bolts of perfectly beautiful and coordinating fabric for my project within minutes."

> Ask for help, you just might make a friend!

Sarah has been helping shoppers select their fabrics for years. Her theory is that it is a lot easier to eliminate fabrics that "just don't go together well" from a big stack of bolts that was compiled quickly.

Decorative threads are a feature in all crazy quilts – select ones that really stand out against your fabrics.

Our tips will help you select the right fabrics.

When trying to select a large number of fabrics for one of the bigger quilts, Sarah's advice is to select five fabrics that you love and look good together. These are your focus fabrics. Now, quickly go through the fabric shop and pull out any fabric that even remotely matches or works with your five fabrics – if you need 20 fabrics for your quilt, pull at least 30 to 40 bolts and then start eliminating.

As surprising as this might sound, it really works. Shoppers agonize about what fabrics to select but find it easy to eliminate certain ones from the group. If you pull the bolts quickly enough, and don't worry about your selections as you are pulling the bolts, you will find this a valuable selection technique – try it. It really works! Once you have a huge stack of bolts pulled, many more than you need, start eliminating the ones that stand out as being odd-looking, or not in sync with the rest. Before you know it you'll have a stack left of gorgeous complementary fabrics!

Another technique that works well is identifying the manufacturer of the fabric, and finding more fabrics in that same manufacturer's line. You can find fabrics made with vastly different prints but the exact same colors, and this is a real treat for adding to your focus fabric. Often a quilt shop employee can help you find fabrics by the same manufacturer.

What not to do: Both of us agree that too much of a good thing is bad. If you have selected a green as a focus fabric, move away from similar greens for your complementary fabrics. If you like the warm colors next to green on the color wheel, go to the soft yellows, oranges, tans, creams and browns or choose much darker or lighter greens and earth tones. If you select a blue for your focus fabric, look at how it contrasts with a white, a cream and a yellow, and choose your fabrics from the grouping that you like best. If you are strongly attracted to a certain style of fabrics, for example florals, force yourself to add a solid and a small scale print in complementary colors. We know that these fabrics will not be ones that you fall in love with, but they will make your focus fabric shine like the center-stage star that it is and will enhance the whole quilt.

These all just blend together – not a good assortment.

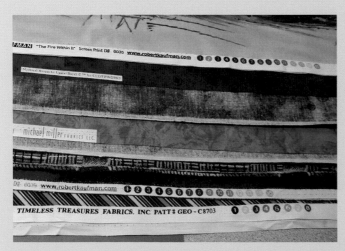

By using the manufacturer information on the selvage edge you can match fabrics that complement each other.

This is a better mix of fabrics with a much better contrast, showing off the beauty in each one.

Selecting Your Backing Fabric

With each quilt design, we provide fabric requirements for the whole quilt, but you have three options. The first is to buy the exact same fabrics for your backing that you are using on the top. So, if your quilt top requires nine fat quarters of fabric and you buy the fabrics in pre-cut fat quarters, you need two fat quarters each of the nine fabrics. If you buy yardage, buy a ½ yard each of nine different fabrics.

You can also buy 18 different fat quarters, using nine for the top squares and nine for the backing. Both of these will give you enough fabric for your top and backing squares. However, you may want to use an entirely different fabric on your back than your top – or, you may choose to repeat one of your top fabrics for the entire back. In this instance, we give you a yardage requirement for the backing only. For instance, a quilt that uses six fat quarters on the top will need 1½ yards of fabric for the back.

Remember that whatever thread colors you use on the top of your quilt will show just as much on the back.

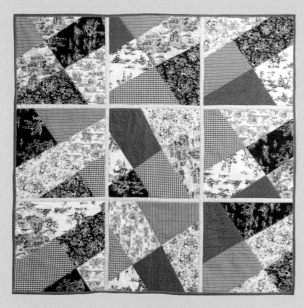

On this quilt we used different fat quarters on the back but kept the continuity of the blue and white colors.

This quilt has a complementary yardage on the back, one that ties in with the gold metallic elements on the top fabrics.

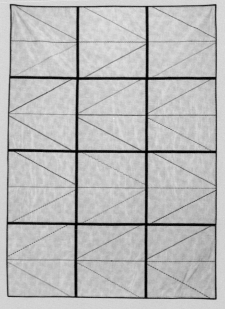

Fabric Preparation

To pre-wash or not is a decision we make on each quilt. If the quilt is intended to be used and washed regularly, we prefer to pre-wash the fabrics, using Synthrapol on batiks and hand-dyed fabrics, and Retayne on all others. These products will prevent bleeding of the color dyes. If the quilt is to be a display quilt, and not regularly handled or used, then we prefer to leave the fabrics unwashed with the manufacturers' stiffeners still intact.

If pre-washing fabrics, we recommend adding sizing or starch when ironing the fabrics after drying. The stiffness helps tremendously when creating the shortcuts and when adding the decorative stitching.

Fancy Fabrics

If you want to use silks, lawns, laces, sheers and other delicate fabrics, we suggest you learn how to best stabilize that fabric and do some practice sewing and cutting before beginning a quilt with any of them.

Heavy-weight fabrics like wools, velvets, corduroy, etc. may stretch more than cottons and may also need a lightweight stabilizer to make them manageable during the cutting and piecing stage of making a Crazy Shortcut Quilt. Your decorative quilting stitches may not show through the heavy nap of thicker fabrics.

Both the thinner and thicker fabrics are awesome to look at, touch and use. We suggest making a smaller quilt to start with before moving on to a larger sized bed quilt if these are the fabrics of your choice.

Quick Bits

When considering fabrics for your quilt project, there are a few basics to remember:

As a general rule – the number of squares in the quilt you are making is the same number of different fabrics that you need to purchase for the top, usually in fat quarter size.

There are two important factors that will give you the look of a crazy quilt – a large number of different fabrics or a large number of cuts.

The scale of your fabric print is important in selecting your cutting design. A large scale print can become totally unrecognizable if cut up five times in the process of making a five-cut design. While this is not necessarily a problem, it is something to be aware of.

If the object of your project is to bring specific colors to the room your quilt will be in, consider using the same fabrics for the top and the back. Whether the quilt is shown top side up or back side showing, the fabrics are consistent with the room décor. Alternatively, you can use one fabric for the entire backing for a very striking look that lets your decorative stitching really stand out.

Crazy Ideas for Selecting Threads

In all of the quilts, thread plays an important part and can tie together all of your fabric color choices. Marguerita loves thread so much that she will make her fabric selections fit the colors on a spool of variegated thread! Sarah likes to use threads that match the fabric colors in her quilt, but she likes "to mix them throughout the project – not match them to their fabric." She likes the overall balance that this brings to the finished quilt.

Consider using some accent colors from your room as the thread color, especially if you choose to use one thread throughout the entire quilt. The mat from a framed photo or artwork, the pot color from a plant, or the trim color from a wall all can be inspirations for your thread color and can create a unified look between your room and your quilt.

As for fibers we love cotton threads, polished cottons, cotton-wrapped polyesters, shimmery 100% polyesters, and we especially love to use rayons for their wonderful sheen. Because rayon is a more delicate thread, we may lighten up the top tension on our machines slightly, and don't hesitate to use either water to lubricate and revitalize it, or sewer's aid. Some quilters find that it helps to keep their rayon threads in a plastic bag in the freezer.

The threads that you use in the bobbin make up the decorative stitching on the back of the quilt, which is just as beautiful as the top. We always match the color of our top thread with its identical colored thread in the bobbin. When using a variegated thread on top, select one color from the spool and match it to a solid color thread for the back, or use the variegated thread on both the top and in the bobbin.

> **Threads are a very important part of any Crazy Quilt!**

You may decide to wait until you have all of your squares cut and re-sewn before selecting your threads. Bring a few of your squares with you to help select the perfect threads.

To help you decide on the number of threads to buy, count the number of seams your cuts have made, counting the entire long cut/seam or the smaller segments that have been created by crossing cuts. You can select just one color thread per cut/seam (for a four cut design that would be four colors of thread) or you may use as many threads as there are segments in the square (each design has a different number of segments). Take a look at some of our quilts and decide how many threads and colors you want to add to your quilt. Remember that your thread choice is an important part of the look of the back of your quilt as well.

Each quilt project relies heavily on beautiful threads. Put as much consideration into your thread selection as you fabric selections.

You can use a different thread for each segment of the cuts.

Or, use one thread per cut as Sarah did on some of the seams in her Beautiful Batiks.

Or, use one variegated thread throughout the quilt for a very elegant look.

If you like the look of bold contrast, consider buying threads dramatically different from your fabric colors but still in your décor color scheme. This makes a very eye catching look in any room!

Not So Crazy Ideas for Selecting Batting

We prefer a thin, needled cotton batting and our favorites are Warm & Natural and Warm & White, because they have a stiffness that gives stability to the square when we are adding our decorative stitches. Your batting must allow for quilting at up to eight inches apart. Be sure to look for this information on the batting package. Some battings only allow quilting up to two inches apart and that won't work for our projects.

If the batting has been tightly packaged and has some wrinkles, drape it over the sofa or spare bed overnight to allow the wrinkles to relax. We don't pre-wash our battings but we have ironed them if they are quite wrinkled, and we do iron all three layers (top square, batting, backing fabric) at several stages in the quilt-making process. For this reason, we do not use polyester batting when making our quilts – we don't want to damage the batting when ironing or pressing.

Be sure that your batting can be quilted up to 8" apart.

Other Shortcut Supplies

For the projects in this book, you will see us using a marvelous tool called a rotary cutter. It is a circular, flat razor blade on a long handle that rolls across the fabrics to cut them like a hot knife through butter. To work with the rotary cutter, you will need a mat to cut on and an acrylic ruler to guide the rotary cutter.

The rotary cutter should be considered a dangerous tool. If you have young children in the house, be sure to purchase a cutter with an automatic cover shield. This type of cutter will expose the blade only when firmly pressed against a hard surface, and when not in use it automatically covers the blade. Please make it your habit to keep the blade covered and your cutter stored safely when not in use.

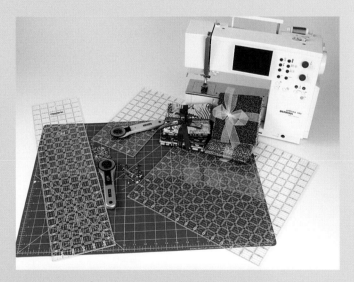

Here are some of the things you need to get started!

In addition to our sewing machine, we will use an iron and pressing surface to press seams flat and to press the sashing. The last tool that we consider a "must have" is a new sewing machine needle for each project. Needles dull easily and should be replaced regularly. Look to your sewing machine's handbook for more information, or follow our lead by using needles in a size 90/14 Q for piecing and decorative stitching.

Our favorite tools are the 15" and 20½" square acrylic rulers. These rulers make trimming so much easier and although not a necessity, they are a timesaver to have. We also love an oversized cutting mat that allows us to cut up to 20" square.

CHAPTER [3]   The Crazy Designs

All of the quilts are created by using squares or rectangles of fabric. You can use the planning instructions we've given or you can create your own – any size square and any number of cuts that you want! The squares are made crazy by making similar cuts through each square, re-sewing them together in a random mix of colors, then adding decorative stitching (crazy quilting). You can have just a few squares, or 20 or more! You can make a few cuts, or many, and each and every one will be unique to you because of the selection of your fabric, the angles of your cuts, variations in thread colors and stitching options in your quilting!

The chapters here are divided into projects that have either three, four, five or six cuts, but please remember the designs are interchangeable! If you see a five cut design that you like and want to make it in the size given for one of the three cut projects, just substitute that cutting design for the one given for the size quilt that you want to have – it's that easy! In a later chapter we even give you instructions for designing and planning your own quilt!

A 3 Short Cut Quilt Design: Asian Inspiration, page 40.

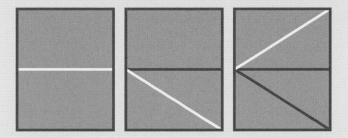

A 4 Short Cut Quilt Design: Think Pink, page 64.

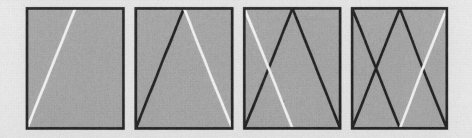

A 5 Short Cut Quilt Design: Fast Friends, page 60.

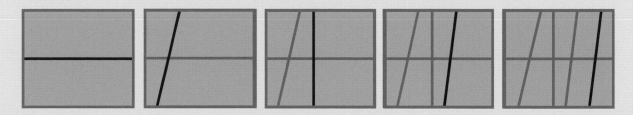

A 6 Short Cut Quilt Design: Warm Chocolate Wrap, page 80.

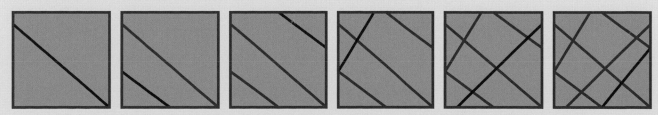

You can adapt any of the projects that we've given or chose to design your own!

CHAPTER [4] *The Shortcuts!*

In this chapter we are going to take you step-by-step through the process of creating the crazy quilt squares. Experienced quilters may be surprised at some of the "shortcuts" we take, so please be sure to review the entire process. Keep in mind that nothing is exact and slight variations are what make each and every quilt unique.

No matter which of the cutting patterns you have chosen, even if you are designing your own cutting pattern, the basic steps are the same:

 Make a straight cut in one square of fabric and use it as the template for making the same cut in all other squares

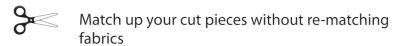 Match up your cut pieces without re-matching fabrics

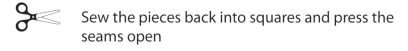 Sew the pieces back into squares and press the seams open

Repeat for as many cuts as your quilt pattern has. As our quilting friend and motivator Karen Tomczak likes to say, "easy squeezie"!

Preparing your fabrics

If you have pre-washed your fabrics, we recommend that you put some sizing or starch back into the fabrics to make the cutting and handling easier. Be sure that all fabrics are pressed flat before cutting. Cut your fabrics to the beginning square or rectangle size that is given for your quilt design, not the finished size in the completed quilt.

Looking at the cutting-line design for your project, place a small safety pin in the upper right-hand corner of each square in an area that will not be cut.

If you are using a rotary cutter for the first time, be sure to review all the manufacturer instructions for use and precautions. We must emphasize how sharp these cutters are and remind you to use caution whenever handling your cutter and to use a thick acrylic ruler as a guide for the cutter and a cutting mat.

If you have purchased extra fabrics for accessory projects, please review the cutting tips in that chapter and leave length in your extra yardage where you'll need it. Consider the final look that you are going for with your accessory projects. Some will require that you create more crazy shortcut squares than are called for in your quilt design like we did with the green Crazy Throw and Pillows, and some will just have you set aside the extra fabric.

By aligning the pins each time you cut, you can be sure you are making the same cut in each fabric square.

Preparing your sewing area

This portion of the quilt making goes so fast that we find it very helpful to create a sewing area that allows us to do several of the steps all at one time. Allow yourself about 3½ minutes per cut, per square. So for a smaller quilt with fewer cuts, this whole process might take 1½ hours – for a larger quilt with more cuts allow for three to four hours. If you are able to have a sewing table, cutting table and pressing area all close by you will find the process even faster.

If your sewing area is a temporary setup, consider some of these space savers: an ironing board makes a good pressing surface, but a pressing pad takes up less space. Have ready several bobbins and a big spool of thread that are a neutral color for your fabrics. We save the decorative threads for where they'll be seen.

Please remember that the height of a dining room table is too high for long term sewing – your shoulders should not be touching your ear lobes while you sew. Relax and if possible, use a low table and comfortable chair for sewing.

It is very important during the crazy quilting process (adding the decorative stitches) that the quilt not have any drag or pull on it. For that reason it is very helpful to have a flat surface all around the needle. Some machines have inset tables that give a flat surface, some come with small tables that give a flat area and there are companies that make larger tables that fit around the arm of a machine. We have also created a flat area by cutting up a box to the shape of the sewing arm and covering it with contact paper. No matter what you use, it helps to have a smooth surface for one foot or more behind the sewing arm and a few inches in front of it as well.

Sarah has a beautiful custom sewing area with lots of extensions but Marguerita's space is limited. Marguerita's advice: "I like to use one or two ironing boards, lowered to sewing table height, along side my sewing table. I set my re-matched fabrics there and can grab them easily to chain piece them together. It makes the sewing process very fast. I love shopping at second-hand stores and I can usually find an ironing board for a good price. I take it home, toss away the covering and use it as a temporary support table when making a quilt. They are fast and easy to set up to a height that works for me and take up little space when being stored."

Create a comfortable ergonomic sewing area with support to hold the bulk of the quilt as you are sewing.

About the cuts in each quilt design

Each quilt gives a cutting diagram, and the cuts are numbered in the order that we suggest you make them in. The sequence will look like this:

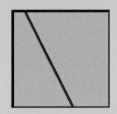

Cut #1

Any slight differences between the angle of cut that the design has and your own cuts is what makes your quilt unique!

You can lay your ruler over the design to get a feel for the angle of the cut if you want to.

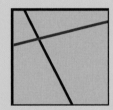

Cut #2

Be sure to review the chapter "Design Your Own" if you want to significantly change the cutting pattern.

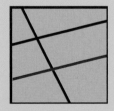

Cut #3

You can make yourself a larger drawing on paper as a guide for your quilt if you want. We will sometimes tape a drawing to the wall next to the cutting mat while making the cuts.

In traditional quilt making each block is squared up (the edges are trimmed up evenly) at each stage of the piecing process. We don't follow this tradition at all.

After the squares are completely cut and fully quilted, **then** trim them, so don't worry about perfect piecing or ragged edges during this part of the sewing!

We recommend cutting one square of fabric only, along the cutting line that your design shows as cut number 1. Then, using one part of the square that you just cut overlay it onto two or three squares layered on each other. Use the first piece as a template and lay your ruler over the edge of the template piece and cut two or three squares of fabric at a time. Experienced fabric cutters can layer and cut their fabrics as they are used to doing for traditional quilt making.

Start by cutting just one square of fabric.

There are no precise measurements, other than consistency in the cutting. We accomplish this by cutting one square and using that cut piece as a template for cuts in all the other squares.

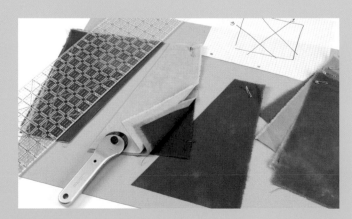

Using a piece of the first square as a template, cut the rest of your fabrics.

Sewing your squares back together

Once you have all of your squares cut, mix and match your cut pieces to re-form squares. Then sew the pieces together, using the chain piece method, making sure not to re-match the exact same fabrics, and using the safety pin in the corner as a guide.

There is absolutely no order to the matching of fabrics – they will be cut and re-pieced several times so don't be nervous! When piecing we use a ¼" seam but perfection is not required! The best standard to use is to be consistent. You can put a piece of masking tape on your sewing machine as a seam guide for piecing. Remember that you may be sewing on the bias grain of the fabrics (the stretchiest angle) and should not pull or stretch the fabrics. As you re-match the pieces, make sure that each set has only one safety pin. This is our guide to prevent sewing the wrong pieces together.

Be sure that you are matching a pinned piece with an unpinned piece.

When re-sewing the squares together, don't back stitch as taught in garment sewing – we don't even pin the pieces together. We layer the two fabrics, right sides together, and sew, feeding them gently with our hands and using a continuous stitch even between sets of fabrics so that when done, we have one long chain of our squares. When you've sewn the last one, just remove the "chain" and snip the stitches between the squares. Sew simple!

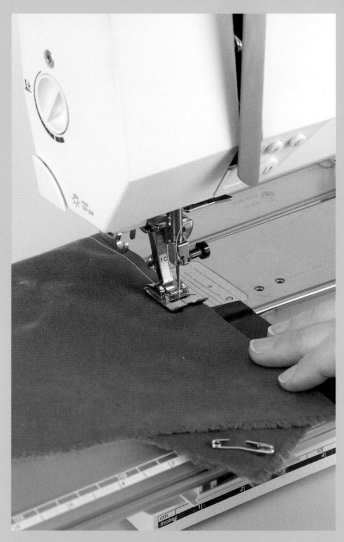

Match the cut edges.

Chain sew the pieces in one long continuous stitch.

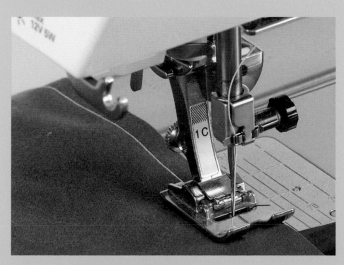

Sew together without backstitching, using eight to ten stitches per inch as your stitch length setting.

Don't stop sewing at the end of each square, just stitch off the end and feed the new seam under the foot.

If you need a seam guide to help keep your seams consistent, try electrical tape.

Press the seams open

After you make each set of cuts and re-piece the fabrics together into squares, press all seams open. This will help reduce the bulk when doing the decorative stitch quilting. Please be sure that you are using your iron to do a quilting press on your seams, using no motion at all. When ironing clothing we sometimes slide the iron over the fabric using motions which actually stretch the fabric. In quilting there is no movement of the iron on the fabric, just a lift up and press down motion of the iron, on and off the fabric, with no movement of the iron while in contact with the fabric.

Press seams open using only a "lift up & press down" motion of the iron.

Follow your quilt's cutting diagram to make cut number two.

Layer your squares for their second cut using the safety pins as a guide – each square should have one safety pin and they should all be in the same corner. Remember that at this stage this is a VERY imprecise quilt and that smidges of differences in the squares is not an issue. Start by making cut #2 in one square only and then, as with the first cut, use the cut piece as a template for cutting the rest of the squares.

Make the rest of the second cuts exactly the same way you did your first, using half of a cut square as a template for the rest of the cuts. You may be cutting right across the seam you just sewed – that's okay, it's what gives the finished quilt the "crazy quilt" look!

The rest of the cuts in your quilt design

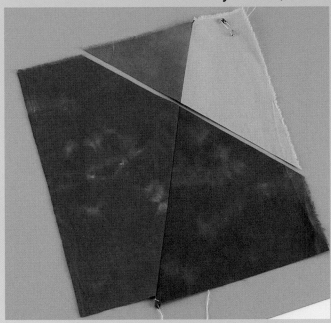

Follow this same process for all the cuts marked on your drawing. The more cuts your design has, the more you "choose" over which fabrics get re-pieced together to re-form a square. Spend a little more time after each cut in re-matching the fabric pieces, balancing colors and light and dark fabrics. Continue to chain piece your squares after each cut, and to press seams open. Remember that the seams in the middle of the squares are not supposed to align and the more that you cut and re-sew, the more ragged and uneven the edges of your square become – that's exactly the look we are going for!

At any time in the cutting process you can change your design, just read our tips in the Design Your Own Square! chapter and cut away!

This rematch has a good balance of light & dark fabrics.

The more the seams are offset and the more uneven the edges of your square, the more of a crazy quilt look you'll have when done!

CHAPTER [5] The Crazy Shortcut Projects

Here are instructions and fabric requirements to make 12 quilts. Each project will tell you the order and angles to make your cuts and gives information specific to a quilt that size.

We ask that you first review the chapter, The Shortcuts, so that you understand the process before you start cutting your fabrics. Please remember that the cuts for the projects are interchangeable, as well as the selection for threads and decorative stitching.

If, as you progress through your project, you chose to change the cutting design at all, first review the chapter, Design Your Own, for tips we have discovered as we have created our quilts.

Once you've made the cuts for your project, please review the Sashing and Crazy Binding chapters for finishing your quilt.

Most of all we ask that you explore your inner inspiration and create your own unique quilt in a completely pleasant process. If sewing time is precious for you, remember that each quilt project breaks down well into 3 sections (of a few hours or less for the smaller quilts).

· the crazy cuts
· the crazy quilting
· the sashing and binding

Easy to Go Crazy!

Marguerita McManus

With only three cuts in nine squares, and using the same color thread for all the decorative stitching, this is a very quick quilt to make. It finishes up at 48" square, making it a perfect sofa throw, lap quilt or room accent piece. It's just right for throwing over a bench to add color to a room, or even as a warm quilt for the car – for those of us who live in cold climates!

I started with a packet of fat quarters from one fabric manufacturer (it had eight fat quarters in it) and then I bought 10 more fat quarters of complementary fabrics to make a total of 18 fat quarters for the top and back – duplicating some fabrics on the back. Some of the backing fabrics were directional and that was an important factor in the final layout of the squares, prior to sashing them together. The ½ yard fabric requirement for just the sashing is very accurate and based upon the full 18" x 40" of usable fabric. Buy ⅔ or ¾ yard if you want excess, or if your yardage is not the full 44" on the bolt. I used a blue binding, after previewing a yellow binding (I just lay out a section of yellow fabric against the edge of the quilt after the squares had been sashed together) and decided that it made the quilt "too yellow."

The crazy cuts took about 1¾ hours; the crazy quilting took less than two hours; trimming and sashing took about 1½ hours and the Crazy Binding took about an hour; so from start to finish, in about 6 hours I had a décor quilt made and draped over the sofa!

Number of Squares: 9
Square Size: 16" x 16"
Finished Size 48" x 48"

This beautiful throw sized quilt took about 6 hours to make!

I used different but complementary fabrics on the back so that no matter which side is up, the beautiful blue and white colors still are part of the room décor.

37

 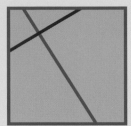 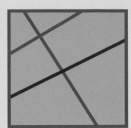

Directions

Cut top, batting and backing fabrics all 18" square to start. Please review The Shortcuts Chapter. For this quilt you will make your cuts using the order and cutting angles shown above.

Once you have your crazy cuts made, without trimming them, please review the Crazy Quilting Chapter for all of our tips on preparing to quilt your squares using decorative stitches. I chose to use only yellow thread on my blue & white fabrics, because I love the combination of blue, white and yellow. For that reason also, I chose to use yellow for the sashing strips. Once your squares are quilted, follow our instructions in the chapter Trimming & Sashing, trimming your squares to 16", and review our cutting diagrams to help you create and sew on your sashing strips. On this quilt, you will need:

# STRIPS	SIZE	FOR
6	2" x 16"	Vertical Top Sashing Strips
6	1¼" x 16"	Vertical Back Sashing Strips
2	2" x 48"	Horizontal Top Sashing Strips
2	1¼" x 48"	Horizontal Back Sashing Strips

Once your squares are sashed, complete your quilt following our instructions in "The Crazy Binding".

Using a yellow thread warmed up the blue and white fabrics and adds a gentle contrast.

Materials

Top Squares	9 fat quarters
Backing Squares	9 fat quarters or 2½ yd. if using all the same fabric
Sashing	½ yd.
Binding	½ yd. or 192"
Sashing & Binding	1 yd.
90"-wide Batting	1¼ yd. or 45"
45"-wide Batting	2⅔ yd. or 90"
Decorative Threads	35-weight rayon yellow*
	Manufacturers: Coats & Clark

Asian Inspiration

Sarah Raffuse

This gorgeous quilt was inspired by both the fabrics and a desire to try very simple linear cuts that don't cross each other in the design. For a really striking look, I went with all black for the sashing, binding and decorative stitching thread.

This three-cut finished out at 51" x 72", a really nice sized decorative throw for any room and really roomy enough for warmth to cuddle up under. The greens, rust, maroon and golden colors are soothing and the straight-line design conveys unity and balance. Many of the fabrics on the top have a "metallic" sheen to them, and I decided to repeat this element on the back, using just one single shimmery gold fabric. This makes a dramatic second quilt with the black sashing and black decorative stitches.

Number of Squares: 12
Square Size: 17" x 18"
Finished Size: 51" x 72"

 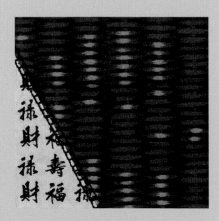 

Using fat quarter bundles of fabric from a single fabric company makes a very well balanced color palette.

A single fabric on the back of the squares creates a stunning backing to any quilt.

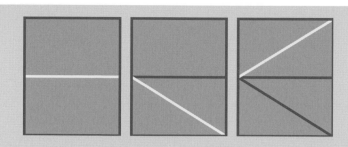

Directions

After first reviewing The Shortcuts chapter, start by cutting your top fabrics in half, widthwise, as shown for cut #1. The original fat quarters are not trimmed, or if your fat quarters are irregular sizes, trim to 18" x 22" the standard size of a fat quarter.

As you make the crazy cuts, as shown above, you will notice that the size is shrinking mostly in one direction. Each cut will reduce the square by ½" along one side making the resulting "square" a rectangle. Cut your backing and batting squares to 18" x 20" and, without trimming the squares, layer for quilting following the directions in the Crazy Quilting chapter. Once the squares are quilted, trim them to rectangles, 17" x 18".

By using the same fabric for the sashing and binding, I was able to cut single strips that were the length of the horizontal sashing - I had 1½ yards in length to work with which is 54" and only needed 51" total length for the horizontal sashing strips. It's nice when that happens because you won't have to piece smaller strips together to make the horizontal sashing. Review the chapter Trimming & Sashing and look at the cutting diagram

to see the layout and cutting order I used for this size quilt. Cut your sashing strips as follows:

# STRIPS	SIZE	FOR
8	2" x 18"	Vertical Top Sashing Strips
8	1¼" x 18"	Vertical Back Sashing Strips
3	2" x 51"	Horizontal Top Sashing Strips
3	1¼" x 51"	Horizontal Back Sashing Strips

I chose to use the decorative stitching only on the seams in the squares and not on the sashing and binding, because the black thread wouldn't show well on the black sashing fabric. A straight stitch made a quick finish and gives a clean, elegant look. To finish off, follow the instructions for the Crazy Binding.

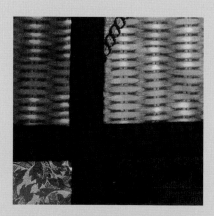
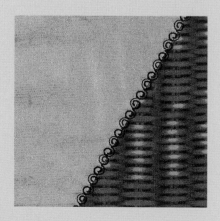

Sarah created a striking design with the black cotton thread and many different stitches.

Materials

Top Squares	12 fat quarters
Backing Squares	12 fat quarters or 3 yd.
Sashing & Binding	1½ yd. based upon 44" bolt - or if the width-of-fabric is less than 44"- 1¾ yd.
90"-wide Batting	1⅔ yd. or 60"
45"-wide Batting	3⅓ yd. or 120"
Decorative Threads	50-weight black cotton

Fossil Fern Flannel

Marguerita McManus

I really cheated on this quilt. I started with a collection of flannel Fossil Fern Fat Eighths (say that three times fast!). By sewing random fat eighths together, I made 12 squares but already had one "cut" done!

I selected these fabrics, not to enhance any particular room décor, but just because I just love the color and mix of fabrics. This would make a wonderful children's quilt, game room throw or car quilt.

I used a Thimbleberries flannel for the backing and I decided to use regular cotton fabric for the sashing and binding, because of the bulk that would result in using flannels. For the quilting I used some of my favorite thread - Sulky silvery grey rayon 40-weight and I also chose to use a variegated cotton thread that combines all the colors of the quilt fabrics. I used just one decorative stitch on this quilt - I wanted to test out the look of a single stitch all over.

Number of Squares: 12
Squares Size: 17" x 17"
Finished Size: 51" x 68"

  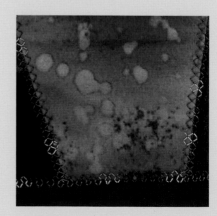

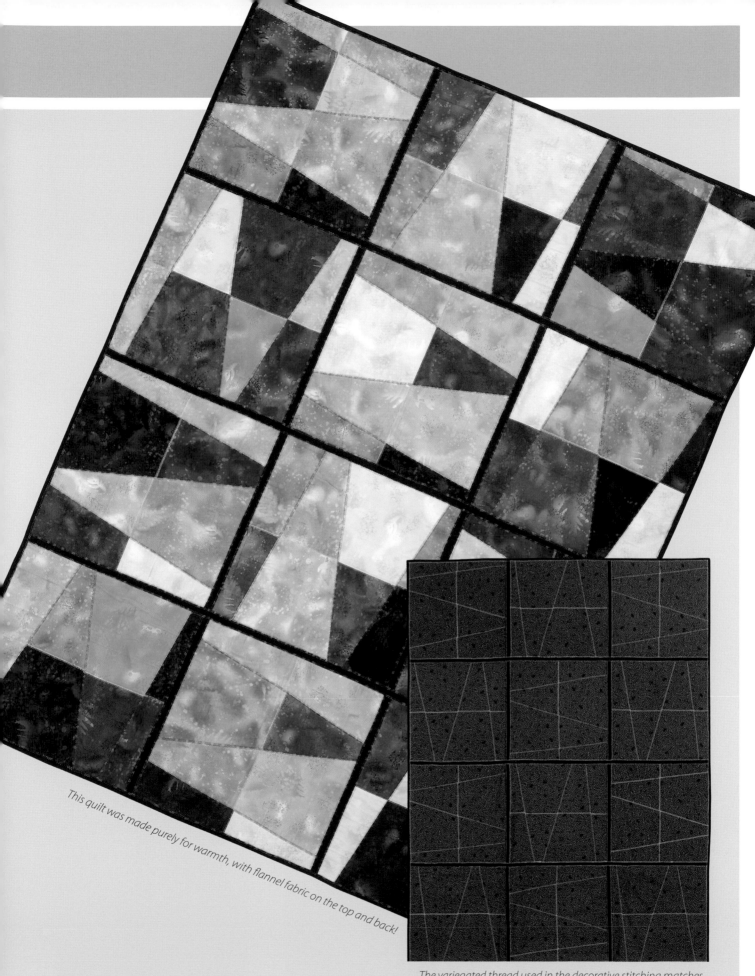

This quilt was made purely for warmth, with flannel fabric on the top and back!

The variegated thread used in the decorative stitching matches the colors in the backing fabric as well as the top.

Fossil Fern Flannel

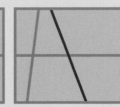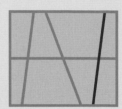

Directions

I never trimmed the original pieces of fabric, just took them as they came. These fat eighths were random sizes, but they averaged 9" x 20". By first joining any two together, along their longest sides, I ended up with rough rectangles. After making the cuts, as shown above, the rectangles became more of a square shape. Take a look at the Crazy Cuts chapter for instructions on building your crazy squares.

When you are ready to quilt your squares, review the Crazy Quilting chapter and cut your backing squares and batting squares 18" x 20". Once you've completed your decorative stitching, trim your quilted squares to 17" square using the directions in Trimming & Sashing. Cut your sashing strips referring to the chart. Flannels tend to be very thick fabrics - great for warmth but bulky when sewing. Please keep this in mind if you make your quilt flannel. Use decorative stitches that are less dense than a satin stitch and consider using a cotton fabric for the sashing and binding as I did with this quilt.

After reviewing the chapter Trimming & Sashing cut the following sashing strips:

# STRIPS	SIZE	FOR
8	2" x 17"	Vertical Top Sashing Strips
8	1¼" x 17"	Vertical Back Sashing Strips
3	2" x 51"	Horizontal Top Sashing Strips
3	1¼" x 51"	Horizontal Back Sashing Strips

When all of your squares are sashed together, refer to The Crazy Binding chapter to finish up!

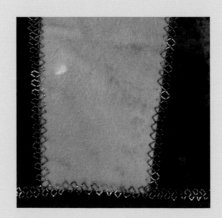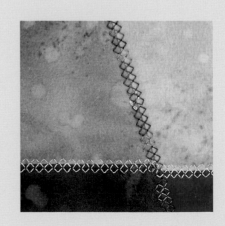

I used my two favorite threads – a silvery rayon in a 40-weight and a variegated cotton.

Materials

Top Squares	24 fat eighths or 12 fat quarters cut in half lengthwise
Backing Squares	12 fat quarters or 3 yd.
Sashing & Binding	1½ yd. based upon 44" bolt or if the width-of-fabric is less than 44" - 1¾ yd.
90"-wide Batting	1½ yd.
45"-wide Batting	3 yd.
Decorative Threads	30-weight cotton variegated and silver 40-weight rayon*

*Manufacturers: Sulky Blendable cotton
   variegated and Sulky Rayon*

Bright Idea

Sarah Raffuse

I am a huge fan of bright fabrics, so when I first saw the Botanical line by Moda I knew I wouldn't be happy until I made a quilt entirely out of that line (picking out all of the brightest ones of course!) When I was trying to decide what to put on the back, I thought the obvious choice was to use the same fabrics as the top since I loved them so much, but a black and white fabric with a very large print caught my eye and I couldn't get it out of my mind. I kept picturing that black and white print with decorative stitching across it in all my favorite bright colors. I decided I had to give it a try, and I used several different colors of rayon thread to do my quilting.

I liked the results so much that I thought the best accent would be to use lots of bright fabric colors in the sashing. Since I had decided on using one color of fabric for the top sashing and binding (a beautiful purple - my favorite color!), I knew that I wouldn't need very much fabric for the back sashing.

It turned out that I had just enough left over from trimming my fat quarters down to squares for the top of the quilt, trimming from 18" x 22" to 18" x 18" left me 4" x 18" in every color of fabric. I cut each of those strips lengthwise three times, cutting off 1¼" off each time - the perfect size for the sashing strips for the back. I used eight of the strips for the vertical sashing strips and joined all of the rest of the strips together to make one really long 1¼" strip and I created my horizontal sashing strips from that.

The bright fabrics turned out beautifully in this pattern, however I think it would work well for any group of fabrics that you really want to show off, because you get a large piece of fabric in the center of every square on the quilt top.

Number of Squares: 12
Square Size: 16" x 16"
Finished Size: 48" x 64"

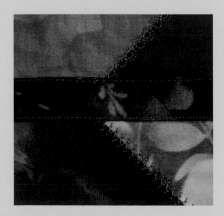
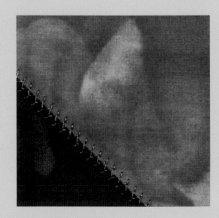

The bright tonal fabrics will bring color and excitement to any room.

The black and white backing is a striking contrast to the top, creating a truly outstanding quilt with the multi-colored decorative stitching and sashing bringing just enough color to liven up the back.

49

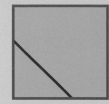  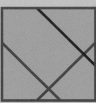 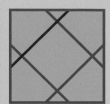

Directions

Cut your top, backing and batting fabrics to 18" x 18" and make your short cuts in the above order using our instructions in The Shortcuts chapter.

When your squares have been cut, layer and add decorative stitches as described in The Crazy Quilting chapter. My decorative stitching in the squares was done with multiple colored 40-weight rayon threads but I chose to use a straight stitch on the sashing and the binding using a variegated thread. Using our guide in Trimming & Sashing trim your squares to 16" x 16" and cut sashing strips as listed here:

# STRIPS	SIZE	FOR
8	2" x 16"	Vertical Top Sashing Strips
8	1¼" x 16"	Vertical Back Sashing Strips
3	2" x 48"	Horizontal Top Sashing Strips
3	1¼" x 48"	Horizontal Back Sashing Strips

Our instructions for a fast machine binding will help you have your quilt finished in no time at all! Please review all of our tips in The Crazy Binding.

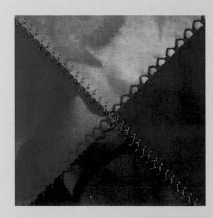  

The bright fabrics and bright threads look beautiful together.

Materials

Top Squares	12 fat quarters
Backing Squares	12 fat quarters or 3 yd.
Sashing & Binding	2 yd. (224" for binding)
90"-wide Batting	1½ yd. or 45"
45"-wide Batting	3 yd. or 90"
Decorative Threads	40-weight rayon and 35-weight variegated rayon*
	Manufacturers: Coats & Clark

Sweet Sixteen

Marguerita McManus

This was a super fun quilt, totally inspired by the fabrics. RJR's Sew You, Sew Fun II line of pop art prints and their coordinating tonal fabrics made me think of a teen bed quilt. Because it was so easy to match up the 16 fabrics, I decided to call it "Sweet Sixteen". I can easily see the fabric as an inspiration for taking a baby girl's room from pastel pink, to contemporary teen, with a quilt, valances and pillows.

The backing is all the same fabrics as used on the top, for a fun reversible look, in a big checkerboard pattern. I wanted a clean, crisp look to the sashing and binding, and decided on white, with no decorative stitching at all, similar to Sarah's Asian Inspiration Quilt.

Number of Squares: 16
Square Size: 15" x 15"
Finished Size 60" x 60"

Update any room with these modern and funky fabrics!

*By keeping the fabrics the same, front and back,
we get a very fun look for any room.*

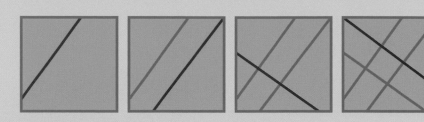

Directions

Start by cutting your top, backing and batting squares 18" x 18" and make the above cuts, bisecting each corner and using the instructions in The Shortcuts. Because all of the cuts are on the bias grain, you should be careful not to pull the fabric out of shape too much, while re-piecing your squares. The nice part of the process is that even if you do get some distortion of the square, it adds to the crazy quilt look!

Layer your squares, batting and backing for quilting as described in The Crazy Quilting, without trimming. With this cutting pattern they may end up very "raggedy edged" when done, but that's okay.

The chapter Trimming & Sashing will show you how to trim the squares, trimming these to 15" x 15" after they are quilted, and you'll need sashing strips as listed here:

# STRIPS	SIZE	FOR
12	2" x 15"	Vertical Top Sashing Strips
12	1¼" x 15"	Vertical Back Sashing Strips
3	2" x 60"	Horizontal Top Sashing Strips
3	1¼" x 60"	Horizontal Back Sashing Strips

Using a straight stitch on the sashing and binding was just a design choice, and you might choose to use a decorative stitch on one or both. See our instructions in The Crazy Binding for sewing on your binding and finishing your quilt.

Using only four different threads and a single decorative stitch made this quilt come together fast.

Materials

Top Squares	16 fat quarters
Backing Squares	16 fat quarters or 4 yd.
Sashing & Binding	2 yd.
90"-wide Batting	2 yd.
45"-wide Batting	4 yd.
Decorative Threads	40-weight* rayon in silver and 3 shades of blue
	Manufacturers: Sulky 40-weight rayon

Double Queen Quilt

Marguerita McManus

I made this beauty from a collection of floral fabrics by Rose & Hubble and a tonal periwinkle blue by Kona Bay and sashing fabric by RJR. The reason I call this a double queen is not just that it fits both a double or queen sized bed, but that when it's reversed it is an incredibly different quilt and amazingly enough, the sashing fabric matches the top fabrics and backing fabric beautifully, giving me two very different quilts. The last amazing thing is that the fabrics, top, sashing and backing, are from three different fabric manufacturers and made years apart. It was just a matter of taking the top fabrics, which I had selected first, to the quilt shop and being open to a lot of fabric opportunities. I had Sarah and Tom helping and I let the experts do what they do best. When Tom pulled out the fabric that ended up being the sashing I immediately said "no, too green, too grey" and set it aside. Sarah picked it up and said "no, it goes with the greens in the florals" and Tom came back with a periwinkle blue rose fabric with touches of green that we all immediately fell in love with. Sarah pointed out that the green tonal went with both the top fat quarters and the beautiful periwinkle blue rose fabric. She counted up the yardage and calculated that there was just enough for the quilt and we were all sold. This was truly a group effort that worked out beautifully. I chose Sulky rayon threads that matched both the top and backing fabrics and got to work.

When planning this quilt I knew that I would have to work on it in sections, quilting for two to four hours at a time, and then setting it aside for the next chance I had to work on it. I had it finished within three weeks, working and traveling in between and enjoying the birth of my new granddaughter, Audrey! The total time for cutting and pressing the squares was six hours, but I divided it up by doing two cuts one day and the other two cuts the next day.

Several days later I was able to start on the decorative stitching for the quilting. I used nine different Sulky rayon 30-weight threads and this part of the quilting used 12 bobbins. I spread this part over several days, using one color thread on at least one section on each square, sometimes on two or three sections (each square has 12 sections). I would sew one or two color threads per day, taking several days to complete this part of the quilt making. I took my time, trying out lots of new stitches on a new sewing machine. I admit that I did a lot of playing with stitches during this process; your timing may be quicker than mine for the crazy quilting - I spent over 14 hours doing 30 squares.

One evening I spent doing the trimming and squaring (about one hour) and two hours working on the layout of the squares, balancing colors and the direction of the stripes in the squares, then pinning on the label tags. I had help again on this portion from Tom, who's eye for color balance is one I've come to rely upon and respect.

Number of Squares: 30
Square Size: 16" x 16"
Finished Size: 80" x 96"

By using very different fabrics for the top and back, yet a complementary sashing and binding, I've created 2 different looks for the bed.

Floral fabrics are a favorite for bed sized quilts.

The gorgeous backing fabric is complemented by a sashing that matches both the top floral fabrics and the tonal backing.

Double Queen Quilt

Directions

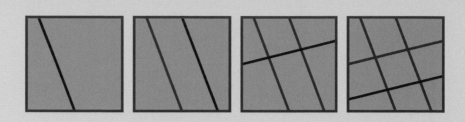

Take your time on a quilt this size, separating the three basic sections into smaller and manageable sections:

- Separate the cuts, doing one or two cuts at a time
- Layering, smoothing and pinning
- Use one thread a day, in two or three places on each square, for the quilting
- Cutting the binding and sashing strips and pressing them
- Sewing the sashing strips on a few at a time and decoratively stitching them as you go
- Adding the horizontal sashing strips and joining one row per day
- Binding only one edge per day
- DONE!

Start this quilt by cutting your top, backing and batting squares 18" x 18". Please review the chapter The Shortcuts and make your cuts as shown above. Once the cuts are made, review The Crazy Quilting for the layering and quilting process, using as many threads and decorative stitches as you want. Once your squares are quilted, trim to 16" x 16" using our techniques in Trimming & Sashing. On this quilt I really loved having a 20½" square ruler - it made the trimming much faster.

For your sashing follow the cutting diagram for a larger sized quilt. Be sure to roll the extra bulk of fabrics as you are doing the decorative stitching on the sashing, and support all of the quilt so that the stitches don't become distorted. Here are the strips that you will need:

# STRIPS	SIZE	FOR
24	2" x 16"	Vertical Top Sashing Strips
24	1¼" x 16"	Vertical Back Sashing Strips
5	2" x 80"	Horizontal Top Sashing Strips
5	1¼" x 80"	Horizontal Back Sashing Strips

Once you have your quilt sashed you are 98% done! Finish up following our instructions in "The Crazy Binding" and in a short time your quilt will be done. Congratulations!

Nine different rayon threads in 40-weight blended well with the top floral fabrics and with the back tonal blue.

Materials

Top Squares	30 fat quarters
Backing Squares	7½ yd.
Sashing	2½ yd.
Binding	1⅓ yd. or 352"
90"-wide Batting	3 yd.
Decorative Threads	9 colors of 40-weight rayon*, 850 yd. spools, for top thread and bobbin
	*Manufacturers: Sulky 40-weight rayon 850 yd. spools

The fabric for this quilt was all picked to coordinate with the pink ribbon fabric in it. I always like to support charitable organizations — and if I can do it by buying fabric I like it even better! This pattern starts out with 18" squares but because of the way the cuts are arranged, the seam allowances make the blocks much smaller in one direction than the other so you end up with rectangles. The finished size for this quilt (38" x 60") makes it perfect for either hanging on your wall as an art quilt or as a cozy lap quilt. This quilt will be donated to the "Quilt Pink" quilt auction that raises funds for the fight against breast cancer.

Number of Squares: 8
Square Size: 15" x 17"
Finished Size: 38" x 60"

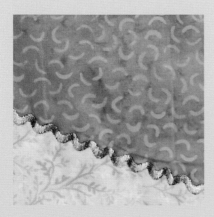

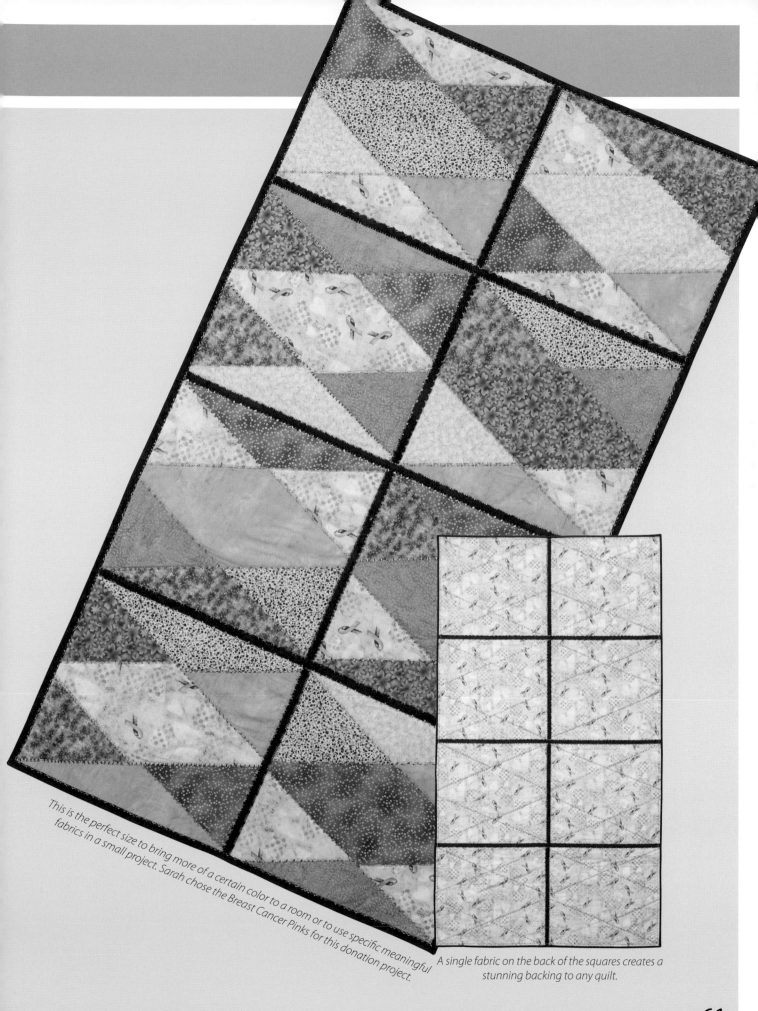

This is the perfect size to bring more of a certain color to a room or to use specific meaningful fabrics in a small project. Sarah chose the Breast Cancer Pinks for this donation project.

A single fabric on the back of the squares creates a stunning backing to any quilt.

61

 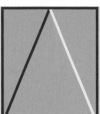 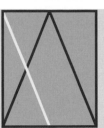 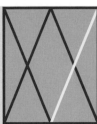

Directions

Begin by cutting your top fabrics, backing and batting to 18" x 18" square and make the cuts shown above in your top fabrics, using our techniques described in The Shortcuts. When you are ready to layer your fabrics for quilting, please review our tips in The Crazy Quilting and have fun! I chose to use only one thread, variegated polyester, but you can use as many as you want.

Follow our instructions in Trimming & Sashing and trim your quilted squares (rectangles) to 15" x 17". For sashing the squares, you will need:

# STRIPS	SIZE	FOR
4	2" x 15"	Vertical Top Sashing Strips
4	1¼" x 15"	Vertical Back Sashing Strips
3	2" x 38"	Horizontal Top Sashing Strips
3	1¼" x 38"	Horizontal Back Sashing Strips

Once your squares are sashed, add binding according to our directions in The Crazy Binding and you're done!

By using one variegated thread and only changing the stitch settings the quilting went super fast!

Materials

Top Squares	8 fat quarters
Backing Squares	8 fat quarters or 2 yd.
Sashing & Binding	1¼ yd. or 196"
90"-wide Batting	1 yd.
45"-wide Batting	2 yd.
Decorative Threads	30-weight poly*, top & bobbin
	*Manufacturers: Signature Pixels

Marguerita McManus

Like the Hawaiian Quilt this is only six squares but is the perfect décor size and with it's coordinating pillows and window valance, brings a warm, elegant updated look to any room. I have been collecting green fabrics (my favorite color) for years and when I received a spool of 12-weight cotton thread in variegated greens, I knew I had a dream come true. I took the spool of thread and unwound quite a bit of it against my white batting and then held every green fabric in my stash up to it – piling up the good matches and setting aside the ones that clashed. What I ended up with was six beautiful green fabrics and a plan. I had enough fabric for pillows and a window valance so I let this be a small quilt with accents, for a color boost to a room that needs some green in it – our living room!

I knew that although the 12-weight thread would stand out beautifully, the stitch would have to be a simple one. The bonus was that the stitching for each square was six to eight minutes! That's fast! I used a heavier cotton thread in the bobbin to balance out the weight of the decorative 12-weight thread. For these projects I actually created eight squares, using six for the quilt and two for the pillows. Please see the Lagniappe chapter for directions on the pillows and a coordinating window valance.

Number of Squares: 6 + 2 for pillows
Square Size: 15" x 17"
Finished Size: 38" x 45"

The top was made using a wide variety of green fabrics collected over the years, made by many different fabric manufacturers.

This fabric is a repeat of one of the fabrics on the top, as is the sashing and binding. The unified greens will enhance any décor no matter how the quilt is displayed.

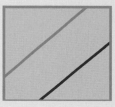
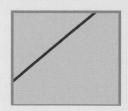

Directions

Cut your backing and batting squares to 18" x 20" and either leave your top fabrics as fat quarters (18" x 22") or cut your yardage to fat quarter size. Using just the top squares, make your cuts in the order shown above, using the instructions in The Shortcuts chapter.

Before doing the layering for the crazy quilting, I did a layout of all the squares to see which ones I liked best for the quilt and which two I wanted to be the pillows. When layering for the quilting, I used the muslin fabric as the backing fabric on the two squares that were going to be pillows — that way I could use the pretty printed backing fabric on the backs of the pillows, where they would show.

Follow the instructions in Trimming & Sashing for trimming only the quilted squares for the quilt into 15" x 17" rectangles. Remember to set aside any squares that you are making into pillows, and trim them later. You'll need the following strips for your quilt sashing, to join the rectangles into a quilt:

# STRIPS	SIZE	FOR
3	2" x 15"	Vertical Top Sashing Strips
3	1¼" x 15"	Vertical Back Sashing Strips
2	2" x 38"	Horizontal Top Sashing Strips
2	1¼" x 38"	Horizontal Back Sashing Strips

Lastly, refer to The Crazy Binding to add machine binding to your quilt.

The 12-weight thread is one of my all time favorites for how beautifully it stands out. The variegated colors unify all the fabric colors in the quilt.

Materials
for green throw with pillows

Top Squares	8 fat quarters
Backing Squares	8 fat quarters or 2 yd. (includes enough for the back of one pillow)
Backing Muslin	½ yd. for the squares used on the pillows
Sashing & Binding	1 yd. for just a 6 square quilt, or 1½ yd. for quilt plus back of one pillow
90"-wide Batting	1¼ yd. or 45"
45"-wide Batting	2 yd. or 72"
Decorative Threads	12-weight cotton Sulky variegated* for top and hunter green * in the the bobbin* *Manufacturers: Sulky variegated, Coats & Clark Star

Fast Friends

Marguerita McManus

This flashy fun quilt is dedicated to my friend Norma, who is going to retire to Hawaii. This is one of the quilts in the book that uses "squares" that are really rectangles because I used 12 oversized fat eighths and joined pairs of them into rectangles. Although the quilt only has six quilted "squares", by using fat eighths I was able to fit 12 different fabrics into the top. I used a collection of bright fat quarters on the back.

I love these fabrics and especially the bright green sashing and binding, thanks again to Tom for his help in selecting the fabric. I had a lot of fun testing stitches on this quilt, using my old sewing machine that has manual cogs for decorative stitching! It has about 13 decorative stitches, but by varying the stitch length and width I was able to create a lot of different looking stitches.

Number of Squares: 6
Square Size: 17" x 20"
Finished Size: 40" x 51"

This is a totally theme inspired quilt – Hawaii here we come!

I used bright tonal fabrics for the back that work well with the top fabrics.

69

Fast Friends

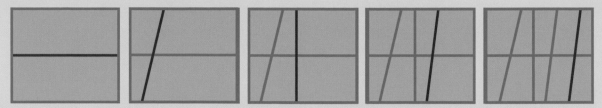

Directions

Start this quilt with 12 fat eighths and pair them together into rectangles, joining them along their longest edges and that counts for cut #1. You can chose to buy 6 fat quarters instead of fat eighths and cut them in half lengthwise using cut #1 as shown above. Continue with the rest of the cuts shown above and following the instructions in The Shortcuts. When you are ready to layer your squares for quilting, refer to The Crazy Quilting chapter and cut your backing and batting squares to 18" x 22". Trim your quilted squares (they are really rectangles) to 17" x 20" using our tips in Trimming & Sashing. For sashing the squares, you will need:

# STRIPS	SIZE	FOR
3	2" x 17"	Vertical Top Sashing Strips
3	1¼" x 17"	Vertical Back Sashing Strips
2	2" x 40"	Horizontal Top Sashing Strips
2	1¼" x 40"	Horizontal Back Sashing Strips

When you have your squares sashed, complete your quilt following our instructions in The Crazy Binding. I loved the combination of the fabrics surrounded with bright green sashing fabric and wanted to continue it in the binding, surrounding the quilt in greenery, just like Hawaii.

All these stitches were created with just one stitch on an old machine. By changing the stitch length and width I was able to create many different looking stitches.

Materials

Top Squares	12 fat eighths
Backing Squares	6 fat quarters or 1½ yd.
Sashing & Binding	1 yd.
90"-wide Batting	1¼ yd. or 45"
45"-wide Batting	2 yd. or 72"
Decorative Threads	Several colors of 35-weight and 40-weight rayon

Beautiful Batiks

Sarah Raffuse

This was my first Crazy Shortcut Quilt and therefore the first time I had to try to pick out 20 fabrics for one quilt. I had always admired the batik style of fabric, and since I was working in a fabric store at the time I got to see every gorgeous new batik fabric that came in. I particularly liked that they always seem to make a beautiful quilt no matter how they are paired. I decided that I should just pick out all of my favorite batiks and put them together — surely if I like them all separately then I will love them all together! That is not always a good motto to use when picking out fabrics, but with batiks it is hard to go wrong. This quilt certainly turned out very nice and ended up winning second place in its category in the 2001 Alaska State Fair.

I picked out six of the colors from the fabrics to match my threads to, and decided to use rayon threads because of their beautiful shine. I tried to use as many different stitches as possible so I would have a truly "crazy" quilt.

Number of Squares: 20
Square Size: 15" x 15"
Finished Size: 60" x 75"

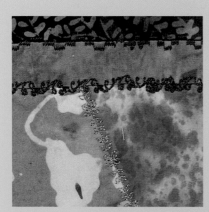  

These beautiful batik fabrics were all the inspiration I needed to create my first Crazy Shortcut Quilt. The variety of colors in the fabrics allowed for the use of many different threads in the quilting.

By using coordinating batiks on the back I attained an overall colorful look.

73

Directions

Begin by cutting your top, backing and batting squares all 18" x 18". Set aside your batting and backing squares, and follow the above cutting order for the top fabric, using the instructions in The Shortcuts chapter. Once your squares are cut, without trimming them, layer and add your decorative stitches as described in The Crazy Quilting. Batik fabrics offer an awesome opportunity for multiple thread colors because of the wide range of colors in each fabric. Use as many different thread colors as your heart desires in the quilting!

We show you how to trim and sash your squares in the Trimming & Sashing chapter, for this quilt you will trim to 15" x 15" square. Be sure to look at the fabric cutting diagram for a larger quilt, it will help you plan your fabric cutting for the binding and sashing strips. You'll need the following sashing strips to join your squares:

# STRIPS	SIZE	FOR
15	2" x 15"	Vertical Top Sashing Strips
15	1¼" x 15"	Vertical Back Sashing Strips
4	2" x 60"	Horizontal Top Sashing Strips
4	1¼" x 60"	Horizontal Back Sashing Strips

The Crazy Binding chapter will show you the techniques for putting on a machine binding and finishing it off with decorative stitches. If you have an alphabet feature on your sewing machine, this is a good place to add a message or sign and date your quilt - it will be part of the quilt forever.

I used the alphabet option on my machine to "sign" the quilt and put in a dedication.

The decorative stitching in this quilt made it a ribbon winner at the Alaska State Fair in Palmer!

Materials

Top Squares	20 fat quarters
Backing Squares	20 fat quarters or 5 yd.
Sashing & Binding	2½ yd.
90"-wide Batting	2 yd.
45"-wide Batting	5 yd.
Decorative Threads	10 colors of 30- and 40-weight rayon thread, top and bobbin

Spicy Table Topper and Mats

Marguerita McManus

This was one fun project! I started with a really bright green rayon thread and an idea in mind about using a satin stitch for all the decorative stitching, which I knew would take a lot of time and use a lot of thread. I had been collecting food fabrics, especially hot pepper fabrics because I love spicy hot foods, and I planned out this set. I wanted to use five squares to make the table runner but I wanted to use more than five fabrics. Selecting my 12 favorite fat quarters and leaving them 18" x 22", I made 10 Crazy Shortcut squares and put five into the runner, made four place mats and one hot pad. I used my two very favorite hot peppers fabrics for the backing for a really spicy look. I created a very jumbled look on the squares with the five cuts, and the total piecing and pressing time was 2½ hours.

Because I want the hot pad to be very recognizable from the place mats, I used a different backing fabric, Warm & Natural's Insul-Bright for the batting, and I varied the decorative quilting stitch on the square and it's binding. Before layering any of the squares for the quilting, I did a layout and selected which squares would be the table topper, the place mats and the one to be the hot pad.

Number of Squares: 10
for runner, place mats and hot pad
Square Size: 14" x 19"
Finished Size: 19" x 70"

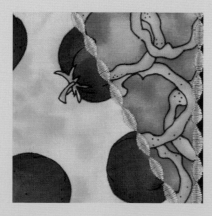

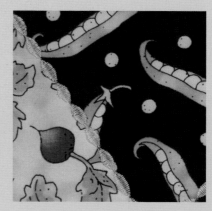

76

Quilted table runner and place mats are a perfect starter project!

A spicy accent fabric changes the whole look! Consider using holiday fabrics on the back.

  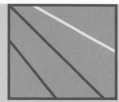 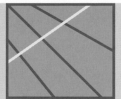 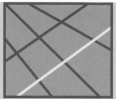

Directions

This project is so flexible because it offers so many opportunities for variety!

You could:
- put a different color thread on each placemat
- put a different decorative stitch on each placemat
- make two table runners so that if one's dirty the other is useable and put different backings on each one
- put a seasonal fabric on the back of the runner
- put different backings on each placemat
- put different binding colors on the mats

Have the kids help select stitches, threads or backing fabrics for "their own" place mat

Start with the full fat quarter size (18" x 22") for your top fabrics and make your five cuts as drawn above. Because there are fewer fabrics (10 fabrics) than sections created by these cuts (12 sections) you will definitely end up with duplicate fabrics in each square as you cut and re-join your pieces. While this is inevitable, you can try not to match identical fabrics next to each other. See the place mat photo and notice there are two sections of the tomato fabric and two sections of the radish fabric on the same mat, but I was able to keep them separated by other fabrics.

Please review The Crazy Quilting chapter for instructions on layering your fabrics and tips on adding the machine decorative stitching. Cut your backing and batting squares to 18" x 20". On this project each square took approximately 30 minutes to decoratively quilt and I used almost two full spools of 850-yard 40-weight rayon thread. The time it took was worth it because I knew these mats and table topper would get a lot of scrutiny and I wanted

them to look outstanding. Because of the heavy stitching in this project, I used two sewing machine needles, and used about one bobbin of thread per square, including the decorative stitching on the binding.

You will only need to add sashing to four squares to join them into a runner. Please review the chapter on Trimming & Sashing and cut your sashing strips as follows:

# STRIPS	SIZE	FOR
4	2" x 19"	Top Sashing Strips
4	1¼" x 19"	Back Sashing Strips

Once you have your five squares joined together with sashing, it's time to plan the bindings. When I drafted this design, I realized that there is a lot of binding in this project, and I wanted to make it as easy as possible to bind all the mats as well as the table topper. I decided to cut the binding strips in one length of fabric, two yards long. Using a solid black fabric, I cut my strips on the lengthwise grain. Each mat needs 67" of binding as it's finished, and by using a two-yard strip (72") I knew I'd have enough at the ends to make the final joining seam. It worked like a breeze!

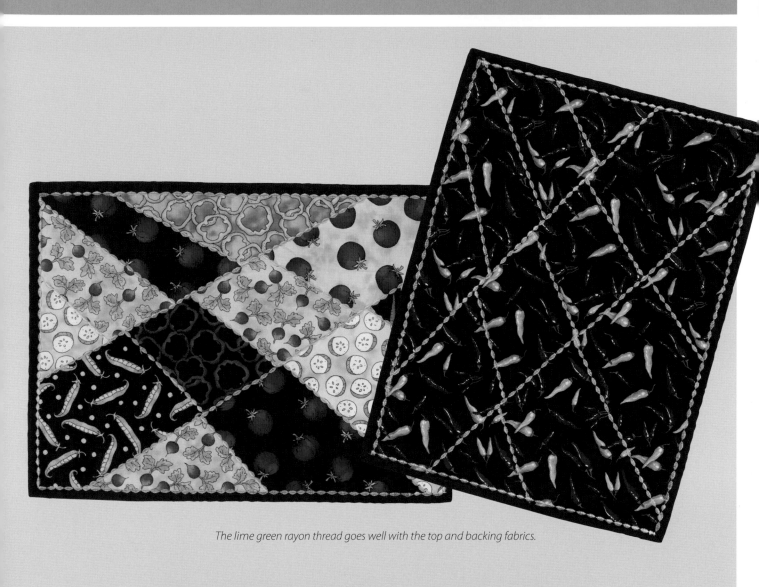

The lime green rayon thread goes well with the top and backing fabrics.

Materials
for topper & mats

Top Squares	10 fat quarters
Backing Squares	10 fat quarters or 2½ yd.
Sashing & Binding	2 yd.
90"-wide Batting	1¼ yd. or 45"
45"-wide Batting	2½ yd.
Insulated Batting	15" x 20" for the hot pad mat
Decorative Threads	2 spools 850 yd. 40-weight rayon*, top and bobbin, using about 10 bobbins to do the satin stitching
	*Manufacturers: Sulky Lime Green #1510

Warm Chocolate Wrap

Marguerita McManus

Although this quilt is small it is a perfect size to bring new colors to existing decor, or to make existing colors in the room really shine. One of the warm chocolate fabrics used in making the top was also used on the sashing and the backing, giving a unified look to the whole quilt.

This quilt is the same layout as Easy to Go Crazy, however with six cuts instead of three there is a greater distribution of fabrics among the squares and lots more stitching.

I used many intricate stitches and six different threads, making the decorative quilting on just the squares a 5½ hour task – much longer than on the three cut quilt, but worth every minute!

Number of Squares: 9
Square Size: 15" x 15"
Finished Size: 45" x 45"

The gorgeous bundle of fabrics from Robert Kaufman was my inspiration to make this quilt.

This fabric kept making me think of melted chocolate! I couldn't wait to finish the quilt and wrap myself up in it!

Warm Chocolate Wrap

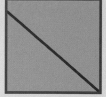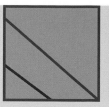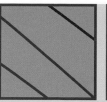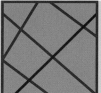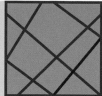

Directions

Begin by cutting top, backing and batting squares 18" x 18". Make your cuts according to the instructions in the chapter The Shortcuts and as diagramed above. Because the cutting diagram creates 12 sections of fabric on each square, but the quilt only uses nine different fabrics there will inevitably be some duplication of fabrics in each square. As you make the cuts and re-piece the fabrics, try not to match up identical fabrics next to each other.

Once the cuts are made, review the chapter The Crazy Quilting and layer your squares with batting and backing and add your decorative stitches. When your squares are quilted, trim to 15" x 15", using the techniques in the Trimming & Sashing chapter. You will need the following sashing strips to join your squares into a quilt:

# STRIPS	SIZE	FOR
6	2" x 15"	Vertical Top Sashing Strips
6	1¼" x 15"	Vertical Back Sashing Strips
2	2" x 45"	Horizontal Top Sashing Strips
2	1¼" x 45"	Horizontal Back Sashing Strips

Finish by reviewing the Crazy Binding chapter and adding your own decorative machine binding. The total time it took to make this quilt was almost twice that of the same-sized three cut quilt, finishing up at just about 11½ hours. It was easily made in a week, doing a portion each day. The fact that it has many more cuts gives it a "crazier" quilt look, but also reduces the size of each square by an inch.

Materials

Top Squares	9 fat quarters
Backing Squares	9 fat quarters or
	If using all the same fabrics 3½ yd. for the backing squares, sashing and binding
90"-wide Batting	1 yd. or 36"
45"-wide Batting	2½ yd. or 90"
Threads	6 different colors of 40-weight rayon, top and bobbin

CHAPTER [7] Design Your Own Square!

We had endless fun creating our cutting designs and you can, too. You can create your own design, decide on what size square you want and make any fabric selection to create a really unique quilt. Your thread options are almost limitless and the stitches your own choice at each stage, making you the designer!

We want to give you some basic information and some tips that we use to help you plan your own design. Have on hand some graph paper and maybe even construction paper, if you want to see how your colors will mix and match.

Draw a square and then play around with some sample cutting lines – each and every quilt is unique. This is a great way to bring children into the planning process, and then into the fabric selection process also.

Tips for the Drafting Process

Here are a few things to remember as you are drafting – things we've learned from experience and that we keep in mind as we design our cuts:

• Don't make the cuts symmetrical – we want the "lopsided" look of a crazy quilt.

• Don't overlap more than two cutting lines – this can make the seams too bulky.

• Try not to create small (1" or so) shapes near the edges; they may end up being trimmed off in the squaring up process.

• Cut your quilted units to a square shape for the finished units even if you started with a rectangle or your "square" finishes up as a rectangle (unless the design specifically calls for a rectangle) – anything else creates too much difficulty with layout and sashing.

• Once you have chosen a cutting design that you like, number each line on the drawing. This will be the order that you make your cuts.

There is a certain amount of shrinkage to the original square size that happens with each cut made as the fabrics are re-sewn into a square. Each cut will use at least ½" of fabric in the re-sewing process. If you start with a square of fabric 18" square and cut it four to five times, decorative stitch it and then trim evenly, expect to end up with a 15" or 16" square once it is trimmed.

When planning your cuts, keep in mind that the fewer the cuts, the faster your project comes together, however the more cuts you have, the more your quilt will look like a traditional crazy quilt.

The number of cuts you make in each square can influence how many fabric segments will be created for the squares. Take a look at the blue and white quilt as an example. It has three cuts in each square and the way that the cutting lines cross each other creates six fabric segments in each square. Because this quilt uses nine different fabrics on the top, there is a good distribution of fabrics among the squares and there is little duplication of fabrics within the squares.

The brown and tan quilt also uses only nine different fabrics on top but with six cuts in every square, crossing lines as we did, we ended up with 12 fabric segments in each square, which means that there are duplications of one or more fabrics in every square.

These are a few factors to keep in mind as you design your own square and plan your quilt size and the number of fabrics that you want to use.

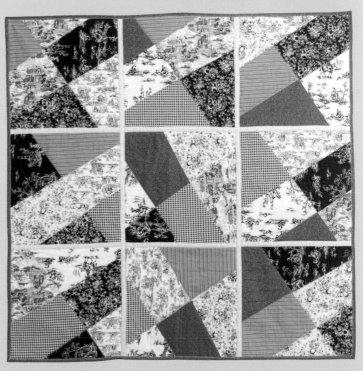

These quilts are very close to the same size, but one quilt had three cuts per square and the other quilt has six cuts per square. Chose a cutting design that gives a look that appeals to you.

Calculating the Yardage You will Need

Calculating fabric needed for the top and back

If you like the size of any of the quilt projects in the book, simply substitute your cutting design for ours, and follow the fabric instructions for the project. This is especially useful for the lap and décor throw sizes of projects that we've done. Bed sizes vary slightly, and the quilts made for them can simply cover the top, or drop over the edges and may include a tuck under the pillow. Generally we round the size quilt we want to the nearest factor of fifteen, so that we can build it with 15" finished sized squares. Here are some common bed sizes and the number of squares that we would use to make the quilt, based on 18" starting squares that are cut to finish 15" x 15":

BED SIZE	TWIN 39" x 75"	DOUBLE/FULL 54" x 75"	QUEEN 60" x 80"	KING 76" x 80"
# Squares in Quilt	20	25	30	36
Quilt Size	60" x 75"	75" x 75"	80" x 90"	90" x 90"
Fat Quarters for Top	20	25	30	36
Fat Quarters for Back	20	25	30	36
½ yd. cuts for Top & Back	20	25	30	36
Yardage for Back	5 yd.	6½ yd.	7½ yd.	9 yd.
Batting (90")	2 yd.	2½ yd.	3 yd.	4 yd.
Sashing Fabric	2 yd.	2½ yd.	2½ yd.	3 yd.
Binding Fabric	¾ yd.	1 yd.	1⅓ yd.	1½ yd.

The formula for calculating yardage for the top of a quilt, if using fat quarters, is: the number of squares in the top is the number of fat quarters to buy.

If you want your backing to have the same fabrics as the top of your quilt, you can buy fabrics in ½ yard pieces, for squares up to 18". By doing this you will have a piece of fabric that is approximately 18" x 44". That is the size of two fat quarters, and therefore is enough for a backing square as well as a top square. The quantity of ½ yard cuts to buy is the same as the number of squares in your quilt.

If you would rather use one fabric for the entire backing, as we did with the Bright Idea, Asian Inspiration, Fossil Fern Flannel or the Double Queen Quilt, the formula for the backing yardage is: number of squares in quilt divided by four. A four square quilt needs one yard of fabric for backing, a six square quilt needs 1½ yards and a 20 square quilt needs five yards. Before you buy, remember that we haven't calculated sashing or binding fabric needs, that's next.

Calculating Sashing Yardage

In order to calculate the sashing yardage for any size quilt, it is necessary to understand exactly how we use the sashing to connect the squares. Please review the sashing chapter, especially the diagrams. There are many options in planning your sashing:

- Use one of the same fabrics as in the top of the quilt as on the Crazy Throw.

- Use a completely separate fabrics as on Easy to Go Crazy.

- Use the same fabric as the backing as on the Warm Chocolate Quilt.

First we offer a very generous measurement here, with the calculations and specifics: purchase one yard of fabric for every 10 squares in your quilt, based upon a 15" finished square. If you want to use the same fabric for the binding, increase the yardage by ½ yard for every 10 squares of the quilt.

Because we prefer to use the lengthwise grain for all of our sashing strips, we tend to buy more yardage than if it were to be cut on the crosswise grain, but we consider this to be a good investment. We save whatever fabric is leftover for our fabric stash, or we make decorative accent items such as pillows or window valances from the left over. Please refer to the Trimming & Sashing chapter for cutting diagrams to get the best cutting layout for your sashing strips, based upon your quilt size.

The vertical sashing strips

For the vertical sashing strips the length of the strip is equal to the height of the square. The number of squares that need vertical sashing strips is the number of squares in each row minus one, times the number of rows. In a nine square quilt, six squares need sashing strips. As an example: Three squares across minus one equals two. Multiply that times the three rows in the quilt and you have six.

There are two parts for all sashing: the top strip which is 2" wide, folded in half lengthwise to 1" wide, and the backing strip which is 1¼" wide. Continuing to use the nine square quilt as an example and using a 15" square as an example, we need six strips 2" wide by 15" long and six strips 1¼" wide by 15" long.

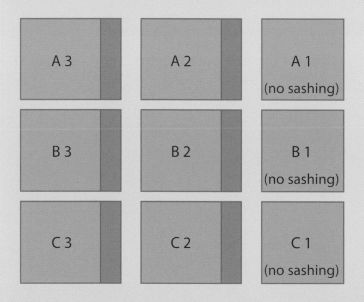

The horizontal sashing strips

While the widths of the sashing strips always stay the same (whether vertical or horizontal) the length of the horizontal sashing is always the length of your row of joined squares, or in other words, it is the width of the finished quilt.

The number of horizontal sashing strips needed is the number of rows in the quilt minus one. As with the vertical sashing, you need strips for both the top (2" width) and back (1¼" width). These should also be cut on the lengthwise grain, however they can be pieced from smaller lengths if you are making a large size quilt. Please review the Trimming & Sashing chapter for our cutting diagrams. The diagrams will give you an example to use as a guide for the layout and cutting of your sashing strips, and from there you can estimate the yardage to buy for your quilt. You will see that for quilts of eight to 12 squares we use 1½ yards of fabric for both the sashing and the binding, and for quilts with between 12 and 20 squares we use 2 yards of fabric. For 20 or greater squares, please use the chart given in this chapter for sashing and binding yardage.

Sarah usually makes the bigger quilts, and her advice is perfect for any quilt of 20 or more squares. Fold your yardage in half, selvages together, and measuring along the selvage edge, cut off exactly the height of your squares. Since our example so far is a 15" finished square, for our example quilt we would cut a strip of fabric 44" x 15". This is the material that you will cut your vertical sashing strips from. The horizontal sashing strips and binding strips are cut from the remainder of the yardage, along the lengthwise grain, parallel to the selvage edges.

Calculating Batting Yardage

We use a rule of thumb measurement for batting, bought at 90" wide – for every five squares in the quilt, buy ½ yard of batting. Remember that we recommend a stiff needled batting that allows for quilting up to 8" apart.

Calculating Binding Yardage

Here's how we calculate binding yardage. Measure and add together the lengths of all four sides of the finished quilt and add at least 10 inches to allow for the final joining section. Next, for a smaller quilt add 10 more inches and for a large quilt add 20 inches, to allow for joining the strips. An example would be a quilt with a finished binding of 192" for a 48" square quilt. We would add 10 inches to allow for the joining on the last connection, and another 10 inches for loss on the rest of the joining seams. We would calculate our purchase of binding fabric on 212".

On fabric that is the full 44" on the bolt, cutting 2½"-wide strips (the width of our binding): ½ yard will give you 288" of fabric strips (not joined) and one yard will give you 576" of fabric strips (not joined). We suggest that you buy a generous amount to be sure that you have enough. We prefer not to use much less than ¾ yard of fabric because it forces us to use the fabric on the crosswise grain (44") instead of the lengthwise grain (27"). If you do cut your strips on the crosswise grain, be sure not to stretch it as you are pressing and folding it, pinning it on the quilt or sewing it on the quilt.

CHAPTER [7] The Crazy Quilting!

Once you have made all of the cuts in your Crazy Shortcut squares, without trimming, it's time to add decorative stitching to them! This is such a breeze because, except for changing threads and selecting stitches, your machine does all the work! When you add the decorative stitching to each square, along every seam line, you are stitching through the square, batting and backing, thereby quilting the quilt. Whether you have an old reliable machine with just a few decorative stitches or a brand new machine with all the newest bells and whistles, we will show you how to pull the best from it and put it on your quilt.

Preparing the Squares

After pressing the last set of seams on your square open, cut backing & batting squares as follows:

Cut the backing squares and batting squares as indicated in your quilt design.

Layer your square, batting and backing together by first placing the backing fabric (right side down) on your table then layering a square of batting over it. Smooth out the batting, then flip the two over and smooth out the backing. Flip again and add the pieced square (face up) on top. Smooth the entire three layers (flipping again, if necessary). Then pin near the center of each fabric, not near or on any seam lines because you will be adding the decorative stitches along the lines.

Cut a batting and backing square for each square of your quilt.

Using your hands and making an "X" motion, smooth each layered square.

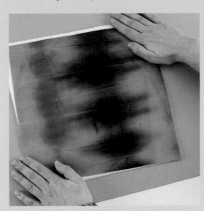

Use at least five pins per square to secure it with the batting and backing.

Flip the squares gently and smooth from the back also.

Don't shortcut the smoothing process. It's important to have very smooth fabrics and batting because all three layers are quilted at this stage. Any wrinkles in the fabrics will be permanently quilted into the quilt.

Use a hard, smooth surface to layer and pin the squares. We like to use our cutting mat — that way we aren't scratching any surfaces with our pins.

Repeat as necessary to be sure the fabrics are wrinkle free..

Preparing for Quilting

Like most projects, preparation can take time but it really pays off. If you have not already made your thread selection, when you go shopping take a few squares with you. We always unwind about a yard of thread from the spool and "puddle" it on our fabrics to check the color against the fabric. What you see on the spool is not always what the thread will look like against the fabric. We use anything from a 12-weight (thicker, heavier) to a 40-weight (thinner) for our quilting and we use whatever composition gives us the look we are going for on each quilt. Rayons and polyesters are shimmery and cottons blend more with cotton fabrics. Thicker threads might make some of the embroidery type of decorative stitches prohibitive because the weight of the thread is too much for a very intense and compact stitch, but they can make a simple and fast stitch really stand out. We love threads and the selection process. They are a very important part of the quilt and, when possible, we've given you the thread information for each quilt that we have made.

We like to match the colors of the top thread to the bobbin in all cases, although with a variegated thread like some of the Sulky Blendables used, we just matched one of the colors on the spool for the back/bobbin thread. Because thread usage varies greatly with the intricacy of each stitch, it is difficult to estimate the amount of thread each quilt will use. Wind at least one matching color bobbin for every color of top thread that you plan on using. Marguerita prefers to use cottons in the bobbin, but Sarah likes to use the exact same thread in the bobbin that she uses on the top, whether rayon, polyester or cotton.

Your choice for the number of colors of thread to use on each quilt is unlimited. Because of the randomness of the cuts, you may have many short sections of seam lines on each square and you may choose to use a different color thread on each one. While changing threads can take time, we've got some hints for you to speed up the process. Don't limit yourself on colors of threads and remember that the thread can change the overall look of a quilt. Also, don't try to match the color of thread to the same color fabrics on the segment you are quilting. You want contrast on the segments but coordination with the quilt overall. For the Floral Queen we matched the colors of the threads to colors in the fabrics, but didn't sew the same color thread to its coordinating color fabric.

Threads are an outstanding contributor to the beauty of these quilts.

If you have set your project aside for any length of time, re-check that all fabrics are pressed flat and the seams are still pressed open.

Remember to have the correct foot and needle plate on your machine before starting your decorative stitching.

Decorative Stitch Quilting

Because it takes time to change thread and bobbin, we have our own shortcut for the quilting. Instead of fully quilting one square, changing the thread and bobbin several times, we put a seam of stitching in one color thread on each square, working through the entire stack of squares, then change threads and repeat.

Begin your decorative machine quilting on any short seams first, starting from the center of the square and working toward the edge of the fabric. Decorative stitching the longer seams last will anchor the ends of the short seams. and will prevent puckers from forming in the backing fabric.

As you look at each square in preparation for quilting, look for fabrics that contrast with the thread you are using. While overall the threads you've chosen may blend with the fabrics, we want to place the threads on fabrics that will let the stitching stand out.

We always bring up the bobbin thread before beginning quilting, and we rarely backstitch. To bring up the bobbin thread, lower the presser foot and take one stitch and then lift the presser foot and slide the quilt about two to three inches sideways. Gently pull the loop of the bobbin thread until the cut end of it is brought up. Put the quilt square back into position, pull both threads tight, lower the foot and begin stitching, with both loose thread ends pointing away from the needle. This prevents the bobbin thread from becoming caught up in the decorative stitches and creating unwanted tension, or from being caught up in the race of the sewing machine and causing a huge knot of threads or thread breakage. It is a good habit to learn for almost all quilting.

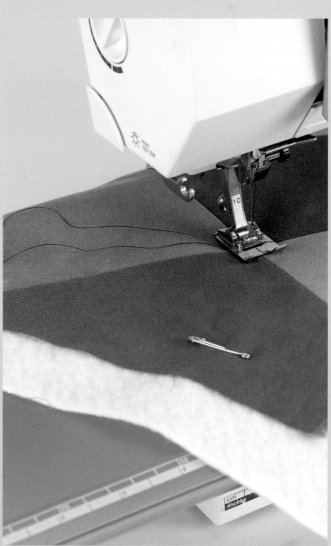

Always pull the loose end of the bobbin thread to the top of the quilt before decoratively stitching.

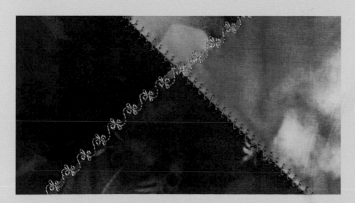

Quilt short segments in the center of the square first, starting from the center and sewing toward the edge.

93

This is really an opportunity to have fun with your quilt making. Kids and other family members can help select stitches and even thread colors. Because the machine is doing all the work, you can even let a "little sewer" sit at the machine and operate the foot pedal. Have fun selecting the stitches – use every single one that your machine has. If you are unsure of the look of a stitch, use a scrap piece of fabric, layered with batting just like your quilt square, and preview the stitch on the scrap before using it on your quilt square. Use this method to check tension on the threads whenever you change them.

Remember that your stitch choice and thread colors will also be visible on the back of your quilt.

These stitches were all made with one decorative stitch selection on the machine but by varying the stitch width and stitch length settings I was able to create the look of many different stitches.

The thread colors on this look just as beautiful against the backing fabric as they do on the top.

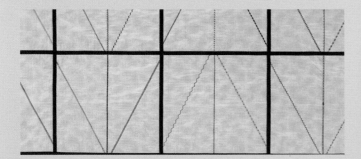

Thread color can make the stitching really stand out!

Don't let the style of your machine inhibit your stitch selection process. Marguerita's 20 year old machine uses mechanical cogs and has only 13 decorative stitches. By varying stitch width and length she can get up to 30 very different looking stitches from this machine. You don't have to own a computerized machine with 1,000 decorative stitches! If you do get started using them all on your Crazy Shortcut Quilt!

Try using every stitch your sewing machine has!

94

We quilted this quilt with just one decorative stitch, but used many threads

Sarah zipped through this quilt in no time by never changing the thread, and just changing the stitch selection on her sewing machine.

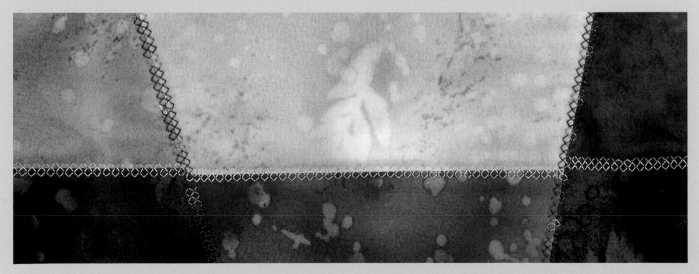

Using a variegated thread gave lots of color with no thread changes!

If you need to quilt an inner section, after quilting all around it, gently lift the square as it is being quilted to ease in any extra fabric.

Lift the square gently if you need to ease in excess fabric to prevent puckers.

If you keep the same stitch from one section to another, or from one square to another, re-set the stitch back to its beginning configuration. Because we stitch right off the edge of the fabric, the decorative stitch may have been halfway through its pattern and might be at a point of backing up several stitches in order to complete its design. By resetting the stitch at the start of a new section of quilting you can be sure that the machine isn't going to begin by backing up.

If you experiment with different stitch lengths and widths, make a note of the settings so that you can repeat that design if desired.

If you are using rayon thread on the top and in the bobbin, make extra sure that the beginning and ending of each segment of decorative quilting is securing the thread ends before trimming loose threads. If the ends are loose, tie a knot in the ends to secure the threads before trimming the excess threads.

In testing your decorative stitches make note of stitches that begin their patterns by backing up. You will need to take this into consideration when using that stitch.

Any drag at all on the quilt can distort the decorative stitch pattern so use a very light touch in guiding the fabric. Be sure you don't have any loose threads on the back and that the bulk of the square or quilt is not pulling or falling off the sewing table, creating tension or drag while you are trying to sew.

By stitching over the thread ends of the short segment stitches, you eliminate the need to backstitch.

If you are not sure if a stitch will anchor or secure the ends of the threads at the beginning of a stitch, bring up the bobbin thread about ⅛" in from the point of the beginning, then slide the quilt back to the beginning point to begin stitching. This will anchor or lock the threads in the same way backstitching would.

Timing Estimates

The length of time that it takes to do the decorative quilting varies with many factors:

- Using a single thread is faster than multiple threads.
- Simple stitches are much faster than "heavy fill" stitches, such as a satin stitch.
- The fewer the cuts in each square, the faster the quilting.
- The more variety in threads increases the time spent quilting.

Specifically, Easy to Go Crazy has nine squares with three cuts and I used simple stitches and a single thread. It took about 1¼ hours and comes out to about 10 minutes per square. The Double Queen quilt, with four cuts and 30 squares, using nine different rayon threads and many different stitches, took 14 hours to quilt the squares – that's about 28 minutes per square. The Warm Chocolate quilt has nine squares with six cuts and I used many different stitches, some very detailed. It took over 5½ hours to do the decorative stitching, which is about 37 minutes per square.

Using a thick thread with a simple stitch is the fastest of all. A satin stitch will take the longest to quilt. For instance, one square done with a single variegated 12-weight thread and simple stitch (four cuts) took from six to eight minutes to quilt. A square with one thread (five cuts) done in a satin stitch took about 30 minutes per square to quilt.

Troubleshooting

If you break threads or run out of bobbin thread in the middle of a seam of decorative stitching, re-sew the stitch on a scrap until you get to the point of the pattern where the stitching ended on your square, then return to your quilting.

If you experience excessive thread breaking, check the bobbin area for lint and loose threads and re-thread both the top thread and the bobbin. If thread breakage continues, lighten the tension for the top thread and re-try. If the thread continues to break, try a different thread to make sure there are no burrs causing the breakage. Test your needle for burrs or just discard and replace it with a new needle. We will often use a 90/14 quilting or metallic needle. If nothing else works for a rayon, Marguerita will spray it lightly with water, while Sarah prefers to use Sewer's Aide. For any other thread, we will discard it and change it out for another one.

If your spool of thread sits horizontally on the machine, be sure that there are no cuts or burrs on the end of the plastic spool that catch or break the thread. Some spools have a small slice in the plastic to secure the thread end when not in use, and this can catch as the thread comes off the spool, if placed the wrong way on the machine.

CHAPTER [8] Trimming & Sashing

Trim, Layout & Sashing

This is a multiple step process that really brings your project together. After trimming the squares to a uniform size, arrange them in a pleasing pattern of rows, balancing the fabric colors throughout the quilt. Then, marking each square with its layout position, attach vertical sashing strips to the front and back of the squares and use these sashing strips to join the squares together into rows. Using horizontal sashing strips (front and back) join the rows together to finish the quilt top. Because we often use the same fabrics for the binding and sashing, review the binding chapter before beginning to cut your fabric. Often it is easier to cut the binding strips first, horizontal sashing strips next and vertical sashing strips last, even though you will use the vertical strips first.

Trimming

First, sort through your squares to find the smallest square. Make sure that the smallest square is equal to or larger than the size called for in your quilt design. If it is too small, you will need to adjust measurements for your quilt (not the end of the world) and sashing by trimming all the squares to the size of the smallest and reducing the sashing strips to the new measurements.

Before trimming the squares, remove the safety pins used to hold the layers together. This is a good time to double check that all the seams on each square have been decoratively stitched. Set some pins aside to be used in the layout portion, after trimming. If the pins left small puckers in the fabrics, these are easily smoothed out with a warm iron.

This is where we have come to love our large 20½" square ruler, but there are ways to do it with smaller rulers. No matter what ruler you are using, you must cut your squares exactly.

Trimming with one large ruler

Lay your large square ruler over the entire fabric square and slide until the inches corner (marked within the ruler) is directly over where you want your last corner. The ruler should now create a perfect 90-degree corner opposite the measured one. Cut along both sides of the ruler.

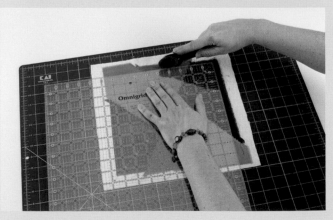

Reposition the ruler so that the newly cut corner is on the inches corner (marked in the center of the ruler) and the cut edges align with the correct inch markings on the ruler. Cut the remaining two sides and repeat for the rest of your quilt squares.

When all the squares are trimmed to the same size, it's time to work on the quilt layout.

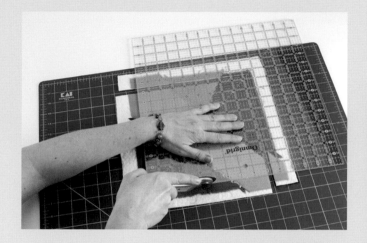

Start by trimming one edge or if using large square ruler, trim two sides at once.

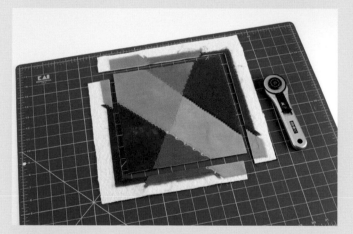

The last cut is the easiest, aligning the top and bottom edges and then verifying that the width is perfect.

Trimming with two rulers

Using two acrylic rotary cutting rulers, measure off a line equal to the final desired size of the square and mark the corners with straight pins, pointing straight down, but not piercing your mat. Using your second ruler, make a 90-degree corner and pin as far along the side as possible. Sliding the longer ruler to the newly marked side, stopping at the pin, mark the third corner. Repeat for the fourth corner and then double check before cutting. Next, cut along the pinned lines to create your trimmed square. Repeat for each square of your quilt.

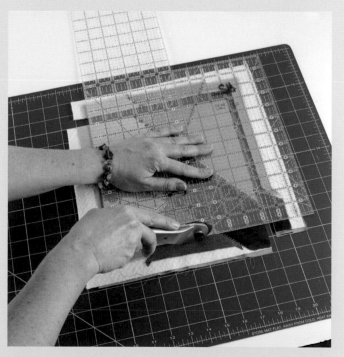

Make sure that you have a perfect 90-degree corner – this part is important.

Layout

The layout of your squares is entirely up to you. Sarah suggests you use a flat surface as big as you have access to and put your squares into rows as shown on the diagram for your quilt design. Look at how your fabrics work together and stand back to find clumps of similar colors. Move the squares around until you have a layout that is pleasing to your eye. Marguerita likes to lay the squares out on the living room floor and then get lots of advice about balancing the color. The more eyes that review the layout, the better! We swap, turn and trade places with the squares until everyone is happy with the layout.

The fabric colors are not well balanced in this layout.

Rearrange your squares until you have a pleasing balance of colors and fabrics throughout the top.

If you used a directional fabric on the back and want to keep the directions uniform, flip each square over to see what direction most of the fabrics are going in. Turn the squares to get the fabrics all going in the same direction. Now, re-flip the squares over, and move them around to get a pleasing layout on top, without rotating the squares. This process reminds me of playing the card game, Concentration.

Once you have a pleasing layout, you need to label each square with a small piece of paper and safety pin.

Starting in the upper right-hand corner of your quilt layout, pin labels indicating that the top row is row A and number the squares working from *right to left*. See the diagram below. Don't pin too close to the edge because we will be sewing on the sashing along these edges. Place your pin and paper about 3" down and 3" in from the upper right corner and it doesn't matter if it's on a seam.

A 5	A 4	A 3	A 2	A 1
B 5	B 4	B 3	B 2	B 1
C 5	C 4	C 3	C 2	C 1
D 5	D 4	D 3	D 2	D 1
E 5	E 4	E 3	E 2	E 1

Label horizontal rows alphabetically and columns numerically

The reason we use a corner is so that you'll know which edge the sashing goes on when you sash the squares together so that you don't loose your layout.

Sashing
Overview of the process

This section is going to show you how to bring your squares together to make a quilt. Our process uses two strips of sashing. A 2" strip on the top and a 1¼" strip on the back to join the squares into rows, and to join the rows into a quilt. This can be confusing at first so please read through the process completely, looking at the examples before you begin cutting or sewing on your sashing strips. It's important to understand the process and to do the steps in order. In this part of the quilt making process, accurate cutting and sewing are important so that the squares join up evenly and the rows match each other.

At this stage you will be alternating between straight stitching the sashing strips on, and decoratively finishing them with the same threads used to do the crazy quilting. Remember to check your bobbin tension when you change threads.

Many of the quilts that we've designed have the same fabric for the binding that was used for sashing the quilt. For the binding and sometimes for the horizontal sashing strips, the lengths of fabric must be joined together in order to obtain the total length needed. It makes sense, therefore, to cut the strips from as long a length of fabric as possible. Also, by using the full length of the yardage for cutting the binding strips and the horizontal sashing strips, we have fewer joining connections to sew and, therefore, less bulky seams as we are doing the decorative stitching.

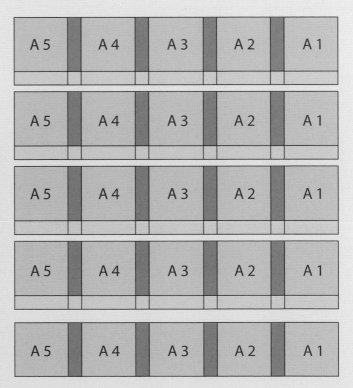

Vertical sashing strips are sewn on first, to join the squares into rows.

Horizontal sashing is sewn onto the rows to join them into a quilt.

The basic steps:

- Cut sashing strips for the vertical and horizontal sashing and possibly binding.
- Pin on and sew on vertical sashing to the top and back of squares – except squares with #1.
- Join the squares to create a row.
- Add decorative stitching with special threads to both sides of each vertical sashing strip.
- Sew on the horizontal sashing to the top and back of all but the bottom row of squares.
- Join the rows to make a whole quilt.
- Add decorative stitching to the horizontal sashing.

We've put the steps in this specific order because certain steps, like the decorative quilting on the vertical sashing, must be completed before the next step is taken.

Cutting the sashing strips

With smaller quilts of less than 20 squares, we like to use the entire length of the sashing fabric for the horizontal sashing and binding. For quilts of 20-30 squares, it is easier to first cut off a length of fabric equal to the length of the vertical sashing strips, set it aside, and then cut the horizontal sashing and binding strips from the remainder of the fabric. Please see the cutting examples here:

Inches	18"	Selvage Edges	36"	54"
1–5	These are the 2½"-wide strips for the binding			
6–9	These are the 2"-wide strips for the TOP Horizontal Sashing			
10–11	These are the 1¼"-wide strips for the BACK Horizontal Sashing			
12–14	Vertical Sash strips at 1¼"			
15–18	Vertical Sash strips at 2"			
19–20				

This cutting plan works well for smaller quilts of eight, nine or 12 squares.

This is the FOLDED Edge

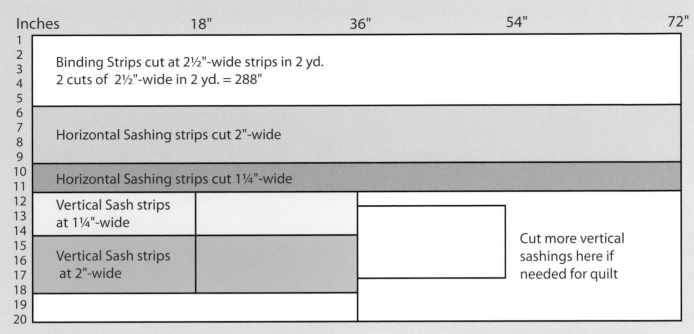

Inches	18"	36"	54"	72"

Binding Strips cut at 2½"-wide strips in 2 yd.
2 cuts of 2½"-wide in 2 yd. = 288"

Horizontal Sashing strips cut 2"-wide

Horizontal Sashing strips cut 1¼"-wide

Vertical Sash strips
at 1¼"-wide

Vertical Sash strips
at 2"-wide

Cut more vertical
sashings here if
needed for quilt

Use this type of cutting layout for quilts of 12 to 20 squares.

At this stage it is important to have precise measurements for your squares and sashing strips. We always cut the sashing and binding strips on the lengthwise grain for minimal stretch along the length of the strip but giving us stretch where we may need it on the width. This will compensate for any slight variances while sewing the strips onto the squares.

Marguerita confesses "The few times that I've deviated and cut my sashing length on the crosswise grain, I've really regretted it. The sashing strips stretched as they were being sewn on and I had to go back and trim them. And, if the square stretched at the same time I had to take the sashing off and re-sew the entire square. It was frustrating, and I realized at that point how much I rely on the stability of the sashing strips to keep my squares from being stretched and distorted while sewing the sashing on."

The vertical sashing

After cutting the sashing strips appropriate for your quilt design, fold your top sashing strips (all strips that are 2" wide) in half, lengthwise with right sides out and press lightly with your iron.

Top sashing is cut 2" and folded lengthwise, back sashing is 1¼".

Not every square will have sashing strips sewn to it. If your quilt only had two squares you would need only one top and one back sashing strip to join the two squares. For that reason, you can set aside the #1 square from each row (ex. A1, B1, C1) and follow the diagram to attach sashing strips to the right side of the rest of the squares.

The top and back sashing strips are pinned on at the same time and we like to pin the squares in each row and then sew them all at one time. Layer with raw edges aligned and right sides of fabrics touching the 1¼" strip to the back and the folded strip on top of the right hand edge of each square. Make sure you are pinning to the edge next to the labeled corner.

Pin all three layers together, with raw edges aligned. Backing strip, quilted square and top folded strip, using several pins.

When all squares are pinned, sew the sashing on using a ¼" seam and piecing thread, not decorative threads. You can chain sew these as well since no backstitching is required. The ends of the stitching will be secured when you sew on the horizontal sashing.

Joining the squares

Once you have all your vertical sashing strips sewn on, it's time to join the quilt squares together into rows. Bring back out all the #1 squares – they get to "join in" also!

Using squares A1 and A2 as an example, you are going to join them using the *back sashing*. Putting the squares back to back but extending the sashing out to meet the edge of A1, pin so that the raw edges align.

The backs of both squares should be touching, and the right-side of the back sashing strip should be touching the back of square A1.

At this stage, pin together and join only two quilt squares at a time.

If your rows have an even number of columns, first pin squares A1 to A2 and A3 to A4. Follow this example for all rows, then stitch a ¼" seam, sewing the back sashing to the back of the square it is pinned to. You can use the chain sewing technique here, too. Don't let the edge of the fabric push you off your ¼" stitching seam.

As you join squares don't let the seam "push" your next seam off track. Keep a ¼" seam in this process.

> Sew all seams in the same direction to prevent distortion or twisting.

If your rows have an odd number of columns, add the #5 squares to the A3/A4 group. Repeat for all rows.

Next, pin the A1/A2 group to the A3/A4 group in the same way as above, pinning the back sashing of A3 to the back of A2. Repeat for all rows and sew with a ¼" seam.

We find it helpful to roll the excess to control the bulk of the quilt.

When you lay your rows out on the table, top side up, the raw edges of the squares should be touching. If they overlap slightly, gently pull the squares apart, stretching the sashing slightly until the edges lay flat and butt each other nicely. This is where it helps to have cut your sashing strips on the lengthwise grain, giving you just a little play in the fabric in the crosswise direction between the squares.

The back is joined and finished but the top sashing is not finished yet.

Finishing the vertical sashing with decorative stitching

The next step is to fold the top sashing strips over the open seams and press. Stitch the folded edge down using a decorative stitch and some of the same threads that you used in the crazy quilting.

You can choose to use a variety of stitches and threads or all the same one! Once this is done, go back and add decorative stitching to the other edge of each top sashing strip. In this step, always stitch in the same direction, rolling the bulk, if necessary. Keep in mind that you are now stitching through up to six layers of fabric in addition to the batting. Some of the more dense stitches may prove difficult with this much fabric under the needle. We prefer to use the simpler stitches at this stage — ones that go sideways and forward, but not backward. We have found that the backward motion stitches are not always easy to sew at this point of the quilting because of the bulk of the fabrics.

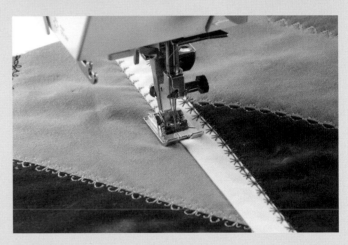

At this stage your project is starting to look and feel like a quilt!

The horizontal sashing

Adding the horizontal sashing strips is very similar to adding the vertical. If your yardage allows for a length-of-grain cut of the entire length of sashing needed, that's wonderful. Otherwise you will have to connect strips to get the length you need for your sashing. We give these instructions here.

Joining horizontal sashing strips

To create your horizontal sashing strips, you may have to join two or more strips of fabric. This is done by sewing a diagonal line across their ends to join them. I like to use a pencil and small ruler to draw a line I can follow for stitching. Trim the excess off to ¼".

With the right sides together, draw a line to mark the seam.

Stitch along the line.

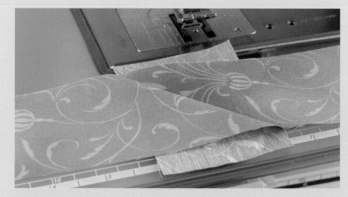

Trim the excess and press seam open.

Once you have your top and back sashing strips joined to the right length (the length of each row of quilt squares), fold and press the top sashing in half lengthwise, remembering to press the joining seams open as you come to them.

Pinning and sewing the horizontal sashing

The rest of the sashing process is the same as the vertical strips for the squares, just longer. Pin each strip of back sashing (1¼" width) to the back of each row along its bottom edge, except for the bottom row, while also pinning the folded top sashing to the exact same rows, just as you did with the vertical sashing. Sew the sashing strips on with a ¼" seam. For this process and when sewing on the binding, we like to open up some small tables or extra ironing boards to "surround" the quilting table so that we have lots of room for the quilt to rest on. Search second-hand shops for old ironing boards and remove their covers – instant table and easy to store away. Stand them up along the left side of the sewing machine table and also to the back side, to catch the quilt as it is being sewn.

Once the sashing strips are sewn onto their rows, you will be joining rows exactly like the vertical sashing. Join row A to B and row C to D. Then join the A/B group to the C/D group. When all rows are joined, press the top sashing over the connection for all of the top sashing and decoratively stitch to secure.

This is the bulkiest part of sewing the quilt. We handle it by rolling the portion that has to go through the throat and by making sure that the quilt has lots of support and doesn't pull on the portion being quilted. We have found that the slightest pull will distort the pattern of the decorative stitches, so we keep a close eye on our quilt and the stitching while adding sashing, but *we don't panic over slight variations!* These are inevitable and only add charm to the quilt.

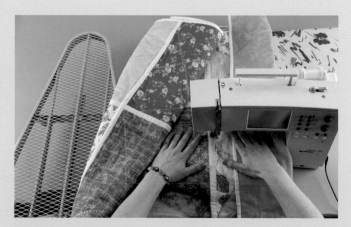

Support the bulk of the quilt at all times to keep your decorative stitches even and balanced.

CHAPTER [9] The Crazy Binding

Our binding is made from 2½"-wide strips, cut on the lengthwise grain and sewn first to the back of the quilt, then folded over onto the front and sewn down using decorative stitches. A traditional binding is cut from the bias grain and stitched to the top, folded over to the back and hand sewn with a blind stitch. You can do a traditional binding if you choose but we love our crazy method. It's fast, beautiful and it ties all of the decorative stitching on the sashing to the binding for a truly gorgeous quilt. We start by making the binding, pinning one side and sewing it on, folding the corner, and pinning and sewing the next sides in the same manner.

Each project in the book gives you ample fabric requirements for binding. We have allowed for joining strips and a 10" overlap for joining the final seam.

Because so much of the fabric cutting for our designs is done on the bias grain, and there are no borders to stabilize the outer edges of the squares, it is easy to stretch the sides of the quilt as the binding is being sewn on. For that reason we provide instructions to measure the binding for each side and pin it onto the quilt before sewing it on. Experienced quilters can put the binding on as they normally would or shorten any of the steps we describe.

Working with one long strip of cut and pressed binding and the back of the quilt:

· Measure the binding and the quilt and pin the binding along one edge of the quilt,
· Sew the binding on that edge only.
· Fold the corner of the binding as described and pin to secure it.
· Measure next side of the quilt and binding, and pin them together.
· Repeat to up to the last corner and join loose ends of binding.
· Fold binding over to the top of the quilt.
· Decoratively stitch the binding.

No matter how you look at it, our bindings are lively and beautiful!

Cutting and joining the binding strips

To create your binding strips, you must join two or more strips of fabric. This is done exactly the same as joining the horizontal sashing strips, by sewing a diagonal line across their ends to join them. We like to use a pencil and small ruler to draw a line to follow for stitching. Trim the excess off to ¼".

This is an easy process: lay right-sides together, draw a line and sew it, trim the excess, press seam open.

To create a very long binding, we like to work in the same order to prevent mistakes in the joining process. As we finish joining two pieces, we slide the finished seam to the left until coming to the end of the fabric strip. This is the new bottom piece. Overlay a loose end, right sides together, as shown. Pin and draw the line. Sew the seam and check it, then trim the excess and slide it to the left until the end of the strip. Repeat until all strips are joined.

Once all of the binding strips are joined to the right length (the length of all four sides of the quilt and a generous extra amount to join the last ends), fold and press the binding in half lengthwise, right sides of fabric out. Remember while pressing to first press open the joining seams.

Pinning on the binding

Pinning one end of the binding to a corner of the quilt, measure the length of binding for that edge (according to the finished quilt size for your quilt) and pin that exact length of binding to the back side of the quilt, raw edges aligned. You can lightly mark the measurement on the binding, or use a pin, to be sure that you are working with the correct length. Gently ease or stretch the quilt to correct for any slight differences between your quilt and the binding.

Measure each side of the quilt before pinning on the binding.

Start sewing this section 10" from the corner using a generous ¼" seam and stopping ¼" from the end. The reason for leaving 10" unsewn is that this is the area that we will make the final joining of the binding ends.

Sewing the binding at the corner of the quilt requires the loose end of the binding to be folded twice. We prefer to pin only one side at a time, removing the quilt from the sewing machine at each corner and at the final joining step.

Sew the binding to the back of the quilt first.

Starting at one corner, measure and pin the binding on in clockwise direction. However start sewing 10-15 inches from the corner. The open area is where you'll join ends. Stop sewing ¼" from the end of the quilt. Remove the quilt from the sewing machine and fold the corner as follows:

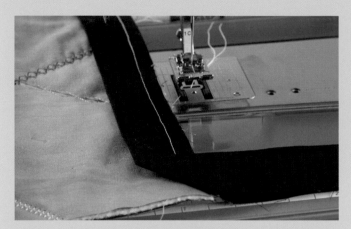

Fold away from the quilt and hold with one pin.

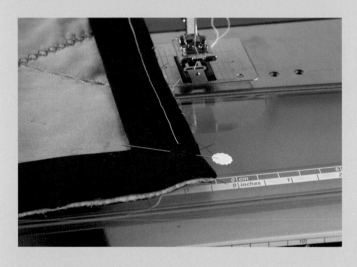

Take the loose end of the binding and fold it away from the quilt as shown above. Place your finger or pin to hold the 45-degree fold just made, and fold the binding back over the corner, creating a straight fold along the edge just sewn, as shown above. Put in one pin to hold the two folds in place, and measure the binding for the next side exactly as done with the first side, however this time begin sewing on top of the folded corner ¼" down from the top. Repeat for all sides until you have folded and taken just a few stitches to secure the last corner.

Now you are back at the beginning 10" gap and it's time to join the loose ends of the binding. Laying the quilt on a flat surface and using a marking pencil that will show on the binding fabric, lay the two loose ends of binding over each other, smoothly. Select a spot in the middle of the gap and mark a dot on all four raw edges of binding, as shown next.

Joining the last ends of the binding is just like any other joining seam.

Fold the binding open and overlay the pieces just like any other joining seam, using the left-hand piece as the bottom, right side of fabric up, and unfolded to its original 2½" size. Take the right-hand binding strip, also unfolded, and lay it over the left-hand binding, matching dots in the upper left hand corner.

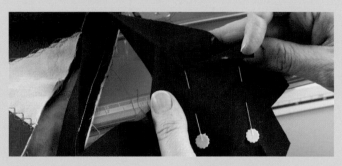

The dots will be facing each other when matched properly.

Pin, drawing a seam line if desired, and sew the seam just as with all other joining seams.

After sewing the seam, gently finger press the seam open without trimming the ends. Hold both ends of the quilt and gently straighten the binding to be sure that the length is correct and that the binding will lay flat and match up to the quilt with no tightness or sag. Trim the seam to ¼" and finger press the seam again, pressing the seam open and pressing it back into a folded binding. Sew the binding to the quilt.

Decoratively stitching the binding to the top

The last bit of decorative stitching will finish up your quilt. Using your decorative threads from quilting your squares, fold the binding up from the back to the top and stitch down with a decorative stitch on your sewing machine. To create a neat fold at the corners, merely fold one binding edge over the other, as shown below.

If you've used rayon thread in the bobbin as well as the top spool, you may have to knot the ends of the threads when you've finished your decorative stitches. I've backstitched and still not anchored the threads at the very end, so after cutting threads, I pull the top thread to the back and tie a knot.

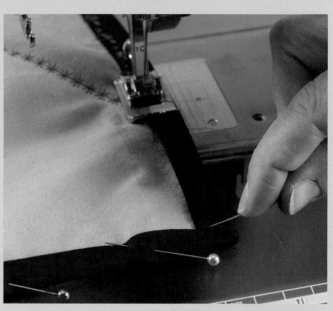

Simply fold one edge over the other and pivot the quilt to turn a corner.

Decorative stitch binding is a cinch!

If your machine has an alphabet feature, this is a super place to sign and date your quilt!

CHAPTER [10]   Décor Lagniappe

Lagniappe is a French word that means "that little bit extra." Here we give you some very simple projects that add the finishing touch to any room décor and will complement your Crazy Shortcut Quilt beautifully. The pillows are simple and stylish, and the window valance is so easy you'll want to make one for every room! Consider using your sashing or binding fabric for these accent items, or one of the fabrics in the top of your quilt project. The valances easily cover and conceal mini-blinds or other existing window treatments, or just add a little extra fabric warmth to your windows.

The pillows can be new pillow forms or you can create covers to fit over existing pillows. The pillow covering patterns we describe are very basic.

Square pillow covers made from yardage

This basic one piece pillow covering is just a folded over envelope for the pillow. It can be removed to be washed or changed with the seasons as part of your summer or winter home decorating.

Materials

Décor fabric to match your Crazy Shortcut Quilt:
        32" x 17½"
Pillow forms new or old, 16" square
Sewing threads

After cutting the fabric, hem each end of the fabric, wrong sides together, with a ½" hem using a complementary thread or one of your decorative threads.

This design simply wraps the pillow form in a single fabric.

Here's where we use up
decorative threads left over from the quilt!

Laying the wrong side of the fabric down and the right side up, fold each hemmed end toward the center of the fabric, until you've made a 17½" square. The hemmed ends will overlap each other. Pin the raw edges in place and sew a generous ¼" seam along the raw edges, backstitching at the beginning and end of each seam.

Fold, sew the seams and turn right side out. Done!

Place the covering over one side of the pillow form and gently fold the flaps over to entirely enclose the pillow.

Square pillow covers from quilt squares

Before using a quilted square from your quilt project, measure the useable size. You will need to purchase or use a pillow form that is smaller by about 1½" than the size of your square. For the example here we had an oversized square and were able to trim it to 17½" square, to fit a 16" pillow form.

If you plan your quilt project from the beginning to include extra crazy quilt squares for pillows, when layering them for quilting you can single out the "pillow squares" and use a muslin for the backing fabric instead of your quilt backing fabric, saving the quilt backing fabric to be used on the back panel of the pillow.

Materials

Crazy Shortcut Square, decoratively quilted and
    not trimmed
½ yd. decor fabric for pillow back
Pillow form, 1½" smaller than square size
Sewing threads

As with the envelope style pillow, page 113 , this pillow cover will have two flaps that overlap on the back. Trim your square to it's largest useable size that is greater than your pillow form by 1½" all the way around. Cut two pieces of fabric for the back panels that are the

The process is a simple one of cut, hem, sew and fold.

same length as your square along one edge, and the length of the square minus 4" on the other edge. For our green square, the back panels were 17½" x 13". Hem each piece of fabric on one of its longest edges with a 1-2" hem. Lay the quilted square right side up and lay each piece of fabric, right sides down, with the hems overlapping in the center of the square and the raw edges aligned with the edges of the quilted square. Sew all four raw edges, using a generous ¼" seam. Turn one pocket of fabric and the quilted square right side out and place the pillow form in the pocket. Squish the pillow, and pull the second fabric layer over the top and smooth out the fabric and re-fluff the pillow, centering it in the pillow cover and you are done!

Sew the pillow flaps onto the right side of the quilted square.

Coordinating Fabric Window Valance

Overview and planning

The valances shown here are very simply made with inexpensive adjustable hanging rods, a fabric stiffener, fusible web and fabric. They are designed to add a warm fabric accent to your room and further enhance your quilt and your décor. You should be able to make your valance in about an half-an-hour to an hour, depending on the size. They are that simple! While a traditional valance is made from wood with complicated angle cuts and a substantial amount of carpentry and work, we've devised a way to make a flat fronted valance from fabric and fabric stiffeners - no wood, no cutting, and no carpentry skills needed!

Each project is designed around the hardware used for it. When looking at your room décor, windows and existing window blinds or curtains, consider your hardware options and plan your project from there.

If you are using your valance to cover existing window hardware (mini blinds, roller shades, curtains), consider whether you will need a specific depth of rod (away from the wall) in order to cover what's already in place and consider where, on either the wall or window frame, you want to mount the hardware. This is important because the measurements for each valance are based upon the final length established for the adjustable rod.

The basic steps to building a fabric valance are:

- Calculate yardages needed based on the hardware length and type of hardware.
- Decide on the width of the valance (height from the top edge to the bottom edge).
- Cut fabrics, stiffener and fusible web.
- Sew corners to stiffener, sew on muslin sleeve to interior of valance.
- Iron fabric and fusible web to stiffener on front of valance, fold over and iron to back.
- Done!

You can create your valance to coordinate with fabrics in your quilt project, or just create a valance in any room to warm the décor!

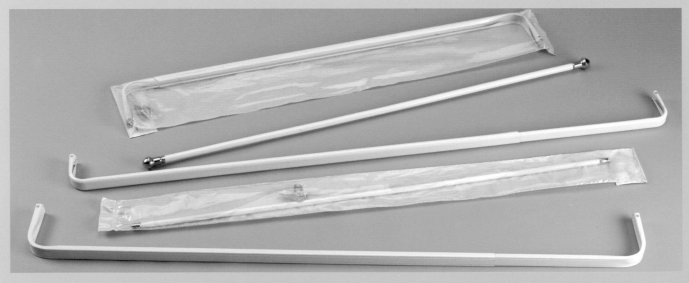

Consider where your hardware will be mounted first in order to determine the exact length of your valance. The flat rod style valance will have corners and sides, but the round rod will just have a panel in front.

Planning your valance

Consider first:

- The width of the window that the valance is for determines the length of the hardware needed to hang the valance.
- Depth needed from the wall, if the valance is meant to cover existing blinds.
- Rod style - a bar rod with wrap around ends or open café style.
- Desired width of valance - the measurement from the top edge to the bottom edge.

As you determine the placement of the valance on your window remember that the valance will hang lower than the rod; by any length you desire, but won't rise above it more than an inch or so.

Materials

Hanging Rod for your valance – we usually find these in the window and curtain section of a home improvement store

Screwdriver or small hammer to attach end brackets to wall

Fabric stiffener

Decorative fabric and about ½ yd. of muslin

Fusible web

Sewing machine and iron

Stiffener comes in 22" widths. If your valances are 7" or less in width, you can create 3 valances from one length of stiffener!!

You can make more than one valance for your window, changing with the season or holidays!

When shopping for your fabric, consider how it is printed on the bolt and if the orientation of the print will work for your valance. Most bolt fabrics are 42"-44" wide, so a valance of total length of 42" or less can use as little as 10" of yardage (fabric cut on the length of the bolt). However, the design printed on the fabric may not work if cut this way. You may need to purchase more than 42" of length of fabric (one yard = 36") to get the straight directional print that you need. Although you may only use 10" cut from the edge of this yardage, there is plenty left over for pillows, shams and other accent pieces.

Fabric is also needed for the sleeve that holds the valance rod – an inexpensive muslin fabric is adequate for this purpose. You will need the same length of muslin that you need of your décor fabric, but it can be cut on the crosswise grain, making it an inexpensive purchase.

You can use the same piecing and decorative threads as used when making your quilt.

Creating a Flat Rod Valance
Measuring and cutting

Because the supporting rod used is adjustable, and comes in different depths, measuring what you need for your window is essential before purchasing or cutting the materials. When you've determined the exact position of your support rod, and ensured that it is going to cover any existing blinds or shades, measure the full length of the rod as sized in place on the window. Add the total number of inches of both of the sides (depth) to the total inches of the front of the rod and you have the minimum yardage to purchase for the valance stiffener. As an example, if your valance is 44"-wide on the front, and the depth from the wall is 3½", the minimum length of stiffener needed is 51". We suggest that you round up to be sure you have enough – we would purchase 60" or 1⅔ yards of each of the materials needed. As you are measuring the length of the support rod on the window, determine the width (top to bottom) desired for your valance. Keep in mind that the valance will rise about 1½" above the rod. We have used 7" for many valances and we like the finished look at this width, but you can chose more or less to suit your décor and tastes.

To calculate the décor fabric needed, add 4" to the length and 4" to the width of the stiffener as determined above. For the muslin you will need a 3"-wide strip the same length of the stiffener purchased.

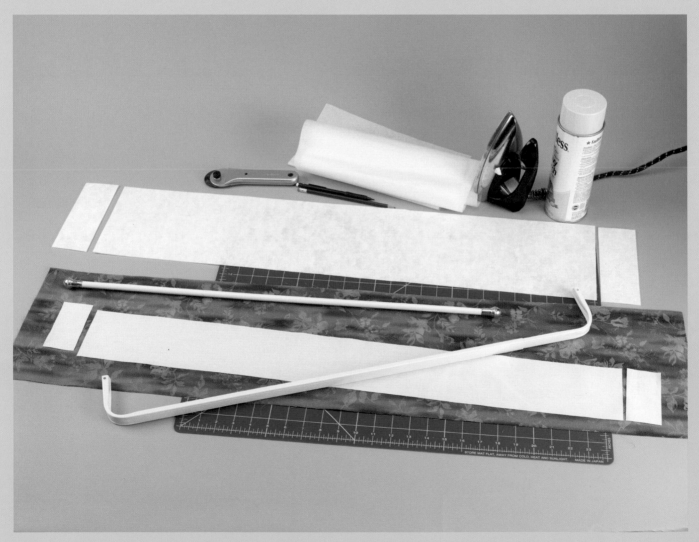

Cut your materials to the length needed for your window valance and the width (height) desired.

The length of fusible web to purchase is slightly more than the length of stiffener purchased. You will cover the stiffener on the full exterior surface, and on a portion of the inside as well, with fusible web. For the back, we will use a 1" strip on the top and bottom edges, and ½" on the sides to adhere the décor fabric to the back of the valance.

Measure out the length of stiffener that you need for the front portion of the valance. Cut the stiffener and then cut the rectangles that will make up the sides of the valance. We like to use the measurement for the depth of the rod minus ¼". So for a valance of 44" on the front panel and a 3½" depth, with a height of 7", we cut three pieces of stiffener, one piece 7" x 44" and two pieces 7" x 3¼".

Cut the main muslin sleeve 3" in width and 2" in length less than the length of the front panel. Cut the side sleeves 1" less than the length on the sides. For the previous example, the front panel muslin will be 3" x 42" for the front panel and 3" x 2¼" on the side panels.

Sewing and ironing

Take a close look at your stiffener and determine which side is flatter or smoother. This will be the side facing the room, with the decorative fabric on it. You may want to mark it lightly with a pencil mark. Do this for the front and the side pieces.

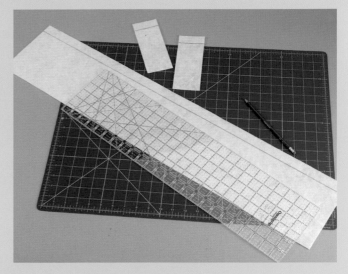

Mark the top edge before sewing.

Measure and pencil in a line exactly 1" from the top of the stiffener, on the inside of the stiffener. Lay the muslin pieces against the pencil mark, and center them on each section – sides and front. Stitch the top edge of the muslin to the stiffener, setting your machine to its longest setting for stitch length. Use a ⅝" seam allowance and stitch very straight. Sew the top edge for all three muslin pieces.

The valance uses an unhemmed muslin sleeve to hold the stiffener in place on the rod. Notice the gap in the muslin between the front and the sides. This is to allow the curved rod to fit in but still create a perfect 90-degree corner with the fabric covered stiffener.

Sew the top edge of the muslin first, with a long stitch length.

119

Fold the muslin up, over the stitched line to the pencil mark and then fold back down again. Press with fingers only, and sew the bottom edge of the muslin pieces while holding the fold in place with your fingers.

By folding the muslin fabric up and back down, we are creating a pouch and allowing for the bulk of the rod.

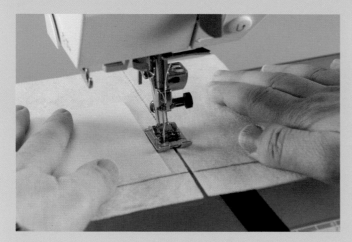

Gently hold the pieces about ⅛" apart while sewing.

Zigzag stitch the end pieces to the front section of the stiffener, leaving a gap in between the pieces. They need to be able to turn a 90-degree corner. No backstitching is necessary for any part of the process, and you can use any color cotton thread.

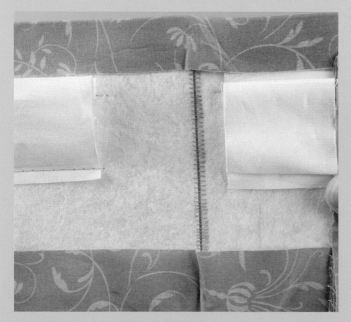

Sew with a zigzag stitch, leaving a gap.

Creating a "pouch" in the muslin assures that the front will remain flat and smooth.

At this point, you can test the look of your unfinished valance by sliding the rod in and holding the valance up in place on your window. Be sure that the valance is long enough to cover any window treatments or existing hardware. The front of the valance should be flat and smooth, and the sleeve should hold the weight of the valance along the top edge so that it hangs straight.

Now it's time to add fabric! Cut your décor fabric, with at least 4" extra length and 4" extra width. Be sure that the fabric is absolutely flat – no wrinkles at all or your valance will have that wrinkle in it permanently. If necessary, iron with sizing or starch to obtain a perfectly flat surface. Cut out the exact size of the front and sides of the valance from the fusible web without removing any of the protective paper. Use household scissors, not good fabric scissors.

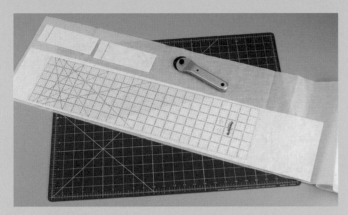

Measure out and cut the fusible web without removing any protective paper. Use paper scissors, not your good fabric scissors. If the glue gums up the scissors, remove with a touch of "Goo-Gone".

When cutting:

Use one full-size piece of fusible web on the front of the valance. Don't try to use smaller pieces.

Be sure that any printed design on the fabric runs straight on your fabric before you adhere it to the stiffener.

Be sure to use a moderate heat setting when fusing to the stiffener. Too hot of a setting will "wrinkle" the stiffener.

Working only with the valance front first, peel one side of your fusible web paper off the front piece of the fusible web and place the glue side of the web onto the stiffener. Remove the second protective paper from the fusible web. Lay the décor fabric over the web, making sure that there is 1½" overlap on the top edge and 2½" overlap on the bottom edge, as well as 2" overlap on each end. Using your hands start at one end of the stiffener and pressing lightly, smooth out any wrinkles in the fabric or the fusible web. Do this several times, going in the same direction each time.

Using a piece of muslin or other pressing cloth, heat set the fusible web with an iron set on medium heat only, pressing from the same end that you smoothed from and moving the iron slowly toward the other end. Set aside to cool.

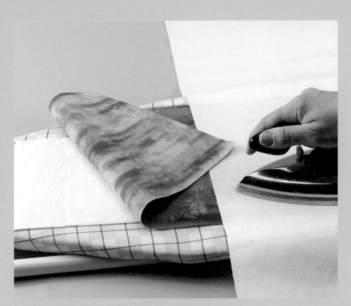

Follow manufacturer's instructions for heat setting the fusible web, using a slow, steady motion and not too high of heat. A too high heat setting can cause permanent wrinkles in the stiffener.

To adhere the décor fabric to the side panels of the stiffener, we first bend the stiffener into its 90-degree angle. With the fusible web placed on the outside portion of the stiffener, bend the stiffener along the zigzagged seam until it rests at 90 degrees. Place just this portion on your ironing surface and let the front of the valance fall toward the floor, keeping the 90-degree angle in place. Gently fold up the décor fabric and smooth it against the web and stiffener. Press exactly as done with the front portion. Do this for both end pieces.

At this point you have some choices about bringing your décor fabric over the edges and onto the back of the valance. There are two simple ways to do this and you can chose whichever one suits your style.

You can sew the edges down, using clear thread. This will leave a stitching line visible on the front of the valance. You can sew the edges down using a contrasting and decorative thread, or you can fuse the edges of the fabric to the back of the valance using no stitching at all.

To sew the edges with thread, work from the back, making sure your decorative thread is in the bobbin, fold the top edge and bottom edge over first and stitch them down, starting and stopping ¼" from the ends. Fold and sew the ends (the edges nearest the sleeve openings) tucking the corners in for a very clean and finished look. Trim the edge fabric to ¼" so that it doesn't overlap the sleeve opening.

You can use fusible web to adhere the ends of your décor fabric to the back. Cut 1" strips of fusible web and lay them along the top and bottom edge of the back of the valance. Bring the top and bottom edges of the décor fabric over and onto the back and heat set into place. Bring the side edges over and trim to ½" so that they don't overlap the opening of the sleeve. Cut strips of fusible web ½" wide and the full length of the edge of the valance. Put the fusible web in place on the stiffener and bring the fabric over onto it, tucking the corners in, then heat set with an iron.

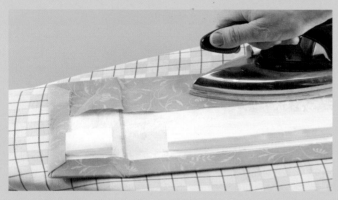

Heat set and done!

Slide in rod, attach mounting hardware to wall or window frame, and hang rod. Start on your next Crazy Shortcut project!

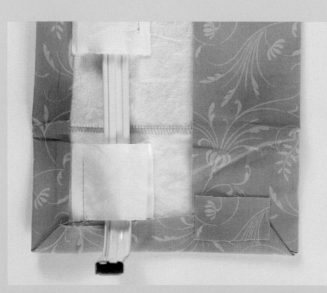

Creating a Round Rod Café Style Valance

Measuring and cutting

Because the supporting rod used is adjustable in length, measuring what you need for your window is essential before purchasing or cutting the materials. When you've determined the exact position of your support rod and ensured that it is going to cover any existing blinds or shades, measure the full length of the rod as sized in place on the window. Remember that the fabric portion of the valance cannot extend in front of the end caps of the rod – to do so would distort the front. There are no side portions to this style valance, making it one of the fastest projects in the book!

Determine the total length of stiffener you will need measure between the decorative end caps of the rod. Decide also on the width (height from top edge to bottom edge) that you want as well. Purchase this amount of stiffener.

To calculate the décor fabric needed, add 4" to the length and 4" to the width of the stiffener as determined above. For the muslin you will need a 3"-wide strip the same length of the stiffener purchased.

The length of fusible web to purchase is slightly more than the length of stiffener purchased. You will cover the stiffener on the full exterior surface, and on a portion of the inside as well. For the back we will use a 1" strip on the top and bottom edges and ½" on the sides, to adhere the fabric to the back of the valance.

Begin creating your valance by cutting your stiffener and fusible web the exact same size. Cut the main muslin sleeve 3" in width and 2" in length less than the length of the valance.

Sewing and ironing

Examine the stiffener to see if one side is smoother than the other. If so, this will be the exterior side that will the room, and you should mark it lightly with a pencil. On the back side of the stiffener, measure and pencil in a line exactly 1" from the top. Lay the muslin sleeve against the pencil mark, and center it on the stiffener. Stitch the top edge of the muslin to the stiffener, setting your machine to its longest setting for stitch length. Use a ⅝" seam allowance and stitch very straight.

Fold the muslin up, over the stitched line, to the pencil mark and then fold back down again. Press with fingers only, and sew the bottom edge of the muslin sleeve.

By folding the muslin fabric up and back down, we are creating a pouch and allowing for the bulk of the rod.

At this point, you can test the look of your unfinished valance by sliding the rod in and holding the valance up in place on your window. Be sure that the valance is long enough to cover any window treatments or existing hardware that you might be trying to hide. The front of the valance should be flat and smooth, and the sleeve should hold the weight of the valance along the top edge so that it hangs straight.

Now it's time to add fabric! Cut your décor fabric, with at least 4" extra length and 4" extra width. Be sure that the fabric is absolutely flat – no wrinkles at all or you valance will have that wrinkle in it permanently. If necessary, iron with sizing or starch to obtain a perfectly flat surface. Cut out the exact size of the front of the valance from the fusible web without removing any of the protective paper. Use household scissors, not good fabric scissors.

Peel one side of your fusible web paper off one side of the fusible web and place the glue side of the web onto the stiffener. Remove the second protective paper from the fusible web. Lay the décor fabric over the web, making sure that there is 1½" overlap on the top edge and 2½" overlap on the bottom edge, as well as overlap on each end. Starting at one end of the stiffener and pressing lightly, smooth out any wrinkles in the fabric or the fusible web. Do this several times, going in the same direction each time.

> Be sure that any printed design on the fabric runs straight on your cut of fabric before you adhere it to the stiffener.

Overlay a layer of muslin or other pressing cloth. Heat set the fusible web with an iron, set on medium heat only, pressing from the same end that you smoothed from and moving the iron slowly toward the other end. Set aside to cool.

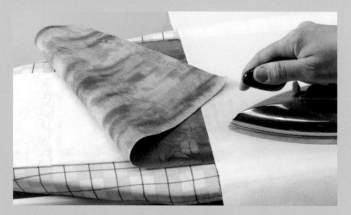

Follow manufacturers instructions for heat setting the fusible web, using a slow, steady motion and not too high of heat. A too high heat setting can cause permanent wrinkles in the stiffener.

You can sew the edges down, using clear thread or use a contrasting and decorative thread. You could also fuse the edges to the back of the valance using no stitching at all or add decorative stitching later.

To sew the edges with thread, work from the back making sure your decorative thread is in the bobbin), fold the top edge and bottom edge over first and stitch them down, starting and stopping ¼" from the ends. Fold and sew the ends, (the edges nearest the sleeve openings) tucking the corners in for a very clean and finished look. Trim the edge fabric to ¼" so that it doesn't overlap the sleeve opening.

You can use fusible web to adhere the ends of your décor fabric to the back. Cut 1" strips of fusible web and lay them along the top and bottom edge of the back of the valance. Bring the top and bottom edges of the décor fabric over and onto the back and heat set into place. Bring the side edges over and trim to ½" so that they don't overlap the opening of the sleeve. Cut strips of fusible web ½" wide and the full length of the edge of the valance. Put the web in place and bring the fabric over onto it, tucking the corners in, then heat set with an iron.

Slide in rod, attach mounting hardware to wall or window frame, and hang rod. Start on your next Crazy Shortcut project!

Heat set and done!

Resources

www.CrazyShortCuts.com

Recommended Reading

The Magic of Crazy Quilting by J. Marsha Michler
Pillows, Cushions and Tuffets by Carol Zentgraf

Fabrics

RJR Fabrics
www.rjrfabrics.com

Robert Kaufman Fabrics
www.robertkaufman.com

Notions

Warm Company
www.warmcompany.com

Omnigrid
www.dritz.com

Timtex
www.timtexstore.com

Threads
Coats & Clark
www.coatsandclark.com

Signature Thread
www.amefird.com

Sulky
www.sulky.com

Superior Threads
www.superiorthreads.com

Other Resources

Sewing/Quilting

Clotilde, LLC
PO Box 7500
Big Sandy, TX 75755-7500
800-772-2891
www.clotilde.com

Connecting Threads
PO Box 870760
Vancouver, WA 98687-7760
800-574-6454
www.ConnectingThreads.com

Home Sew
PO Box 4099
Bethlehem, PA 18018-0099
800-344-4739
www.homesew.com

Nancy's Notions
333 Beichl Ave
PO Box 683
Beaver Dam, WI 53916-0683
800-833-0690
www.nancysnotions.com

Krause Publications
700 E. State St.
Iola, WI 54990
800-258-0929
www.krausebooks.com

Quilting

Keepsake Quilting
Route 25
PO Box 1618
Center Harbor, NH 03226-1618
800-438-5464
www.keepsakequilting.com

Annie's Attic
1 Annie Lane
Big Sandy, TX 75755
800-582-6643
www.anniesattic.com

Marguerita's Bio

Born and raised in New England, Marguerita moved to Alaska in 1978, drawn there by her aunt, Carol Silva. She lived in Anchorage for 22 years and in 2000 moved to Seward, Alaska. She has enjoyed being a mother, aunt, bookkeeper, tax collector, professional longarm quilter, ocean kayaker, commercial fisherman and quilt teacher. She is looking forward to retirement and spending more time writing, teaching, traveling, improving her pool game, fishing with her partner Tom, and spending time with her daughter, Sarah, son-in-law, Ryan, new granddaughter, Audrey and many, many pet rabbits. You may contact Marguerita through www.CrazyShortCuts.com.

Sarah's Bio

Born and raised in Anchorage, Alaska, Sarah started quilting at age 17 under the tutelage of Karen Tomczak at Quilt Works, where she became a quilt teacher and attended International Quilt Market in Houston and Portland. She graduated from Service High School in 2000 and worked with Dina Pappas opening Dina's quilt store in Eagle River, Alaska. Sarah married Ryan Raffuse in 2003 and they had their first child, Audrey Marie, in September 2006. Sarah enjoys being home with her new baby and Ryan manages Anchorage House of Hobbies with his father and grandmother.

Enhance Your Stitchin' Skills

Raggedy Reverse Applique

15+ Fast Fun and Forgiving Projects

by Kim Deneault

Discover a stress-free new appliqué technique in the detailed instructions and 175 color photos and illustrations of this book. Plus, you'll find 12+ projects for small and quick projects, as well as more complex projects, featured on a pattern insert.

Softcover • 8¼ x 10⅞
128 pages • 225 b&w illus.
175 color photos
Item# Z0765 • $24.99

Quilting The Complete Guide

by Darlene Zimmerman

Everything you need to know to quilt is in this book. More than 400 color photos and illustrations demonstrate the quilt making process.

Hardcover • 5⅝ x 7⅝ • 256 pages
400 color photos and illus.
Item# Z0320 • $29.99

Chameleon Quilts

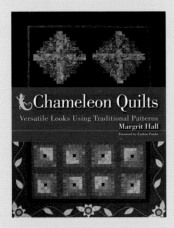

Versatile Looks Using Traditional Patterns

by Margrit Hall,
Foreword by Earlene Fowler

Learn how to use new fabrics, colors and textures and the same set of 10 quilt patterns to create 19 different projects. Features more than 200 step-by-step color photos and graphics.

Softcover • 8¼ x 10⅞
128 pages • 200+ color photos
Item# Z0104 • $22.99

One Stitch™ Quilting: The Basics

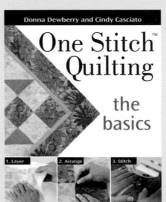

20 Fun Projects You Can Finish in a Day

by Donna Dewberry and Cindy Casciato

Create stylish quilt projects in less time with this innovative new quilting method represented in the more than 300 color photos and illustrations, and demonstrated in 20 exciting projects included in this book.

Softcover • 8¼ x 10⅞
128 pages • 300 color photos
Item# OSQB • $22.99

90-Minute Fabric Fun

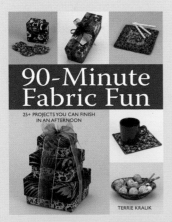

30 Projects You Can Finish in an Afternoon

by Terrie Kralik

Create 30 beautiful projects for the home or to give as gifts including fabric boxes and bowls using fabric techniques explained and and demonstrated in 200 detailed color photos.

Softcover • 8¼ x 10⅞ • 144 pages
200+ color photos and illus.
Item# Z0102 • $24.99

Call 800-258-0929 to Order!

M-F 8am-5pm • Offer CRB7

Krause Publications, Offer **CRB7**
PO Box 5009, Iola WI 54945-5009
www.krausebooks.com

Order directly from the publisher by calling
800-258-0929 M-F 8 am - 5 pm

Online at www.krausebooks.com or from booksellers and craft and fabric shops nationwide.

Please reference offer **CRB7**
with all direct-to-publisher orders.